Chartism

Richard Brown
Manshead School

CAMBRIDGE
UNIVERSITY PRESS

For Julie, 1970–96, a true radical

PUBLISHED BY THE PRESS SYNDICATE OF THE UNIVERSITY OF CAMBRIDGE
The Pitt Building, Trumpington Street, Cambridge, United Kingdom

CAMBRIDGE UNIVERSITY PRESS
The Edinburgh Building, Cambridge CB2 2RU, UK
40 West 20th Street, New York, NY 10011–4211, USA
10 Stamford Road, Oakleigh, VIC 3166, Australia
Ruiz de Alarcón 13, 28014 Madrid, Spain
Dock House, The Waterfront, Cape Town 8001, South Africa

http://www.cambridge.org

First published 1998
Reprinted 2000

Printed in the United Kingdom at the University Press, Cambridge

Typeset in Tiepolo and Formata

A catalogue record for this book is available from the British Library

ISBN 0 521 58617 8 paperback

Text design by Newton Harris

Acknowledgements
Cover, Birmingham Museum and Art Gallery / Bridgeman Art Library, London /
New York; 11, Fotomas Index; 61, The National Library of Wales; 94, 105,
reproduced with permission of Punch Ltd; 108, The Royal Archive Collection
© Her Royal Majesty the Queen.

The cover painting by Benjamin Robert Haydon (1786–1846) shows a meeting of
the Birmingham Political Union.

Contents

Contents

Preface

In December 1847, William Loveless wrote to his brother George, one of the Tolpuddle Martyrs, 'We seek not to be rich in this world's goods – we wish only to work for ourselves so that we may enjoy the fruits of our toil, without being subject to a tyrant master.' Caught in a changing economic and social system, working people in larger numbers than ever before sought through radical agitation to obtain the right to vote. They saw this as a means of obtaining recognition in an unequal society and as the only way in which they could remove the inequalities and injustices of their society. For most, the demand was not for revolutionary change but for fairness, for equality and for economic independence.

This book considers how working people sought justice through the Chartist movement. It poses fundamental questions about the movement and considers them through the eyes of both contemporaries and later historians. The nature and development of Chartism is, at one level, deceptively simple. However, as revisionist historians have shown, the demands of the Charter masked deeper concerns among working people about the direction in which British society was evolving and differences as to how those concerns could be resolved.

It is almost 15 years since Christopher Daniels and I first wrote on the subject of Chartism. Since that time, the ways in which historians view the movement have altered significantly. Chartism is no longer seen as an inevitable part of the development of parliamentary democracy in this country. Yet there are still major gaps in our understanding. This historiographical focus is a significant part of the book, especially in the introductory chapter.

My debt to other historians is obvious. I am particularly grateful to Miles Taylor, whose comments on the typescript I found especially useful.

The Chartists were much concerned with the 'loss' of the world and society in which they were reared. In education today this 'loss' is also evident. The many students whom I have taught in the past decade at Manshead School have made that change easier. Watching them develop their understanding of history has made teaching what it should always be – a pleasure. My debt to them is enormous and continuing.

Finally, there is a debt that can never be repaid. I have been fortunate to have, in Margaret, someone who understands the importance that writing holds for me and who has been willing to allow me to get on with it. Our sense of 'loss' has been sharpened by the death of our daughter in the later stages of writing this book. It is devoted to her memory.

Richard Brown, July 1997

The Six Points
OF THE
PEOPLE'S
CHARTER.

1. A VOTE for every man twenty-one years of age, of sound mind, and not undergoing punishment for crime.

2. THE BALLOT.—To protect the elector in the exercise of his vote.

3. NO PROPERTY QUALIFICATION for Members of Parliament—thus enabling the constituencies to return the man of their choice, be he rich or poor.

4. PAYMENT OF MEMBERS, Thus enabling an honest tradesman, working man, or other person, to serve a constituency, when taken from his business to attend the interests of the country.

5. EQUAL CONSTITUENCIES, securing the same amount of representation for the same number of electors, instead of allowing small constituencies to swamp the votes of large ones.

6. ANNUAL PARLIAMENTS, thus presenting the most effectual check to bribery and intimidation, since though a constituency might be bought once in seven years (even with the ballot), no purse could buy a constituency (under a system of universal suffrage) in each ensuing twelvemonth; and since members, when elected for a year only, would not be able to defy and betray their constituents as now.

Introduction:
Chartism – a question of interpretation

Between 1838 and 1858, large sections of the working classes of Britain were involved in the Chartist movement. On three occasions during that time – in 1839, 1842 and 1848 – extensive national campaigns took place and signatures were collected for national petitions calling for universal suffrage. These were presented to parliament and on each occasion they were rejected. Understanding Chartism seems deceptively simple: it was a widespread campaign among working people between 1838 and 1858 which failed to achieve any of its political demands. In their work, *The bleak age*, J. L. and Barbara Hammond wrote that the history of the Chartist movement was 'confused and perplexing'. Yet, as J. F. C. Harrison, a more recent historian, said: 'For nearly twenty years after 1837, Chartism was a name to evoke the wildest hopes and worst fears, like Bolshevism in a later age.'[1]

Why did the movement fascinate its contemporaries and later writers alike? Firstly, the Chartists wanted to reform society by changing the way in which they were governed. Chartism maintained that the lives of ordinary people could not be improved without their right to vote. Secondly, Chartism addressed questions that were later to challenge the modern labour movement. How, for example, is it possible to implement particular political principles? What methods should be employed? Is change something that could be better achieved dramatically through revolution or by more gradual means? How can the support of working people be obtained and, more importantly, retained over time? Finally, there is a crucial historiographical dimension: many who have written about the movement have either been looking for the origins of their personal political beliefs or have used Chartism as a means of assessing their own historical theories. As a result, the interpretation of Chartism is closely connected with the understanding of events in the writers' own worlds. This has affected their perception of Chartism and its influence.[2]

Contemporary writers and early historians, 1850–80

Nineteenth-century society unquestionably saw itself as a society of different 'classes'. What this meant in practice was a cause of considerable contemporary debate. Some people argued that there were two classes: William Cobbett, for example, saw society in terms of 'masters and slaves'; Karl Marx and Friedrich Engels recognised the proletariat and the bourgeoisie;[3] Benjamin Disraeli saw 'two nations', the rich and the poor.[4] Other writers perceived three or more classes. The crucial point is that, whether modern historians like it or not, we

1

cannot get away from the fact that the contemporaries of Chartism regarded their society as one based on class and that contemporary definitions of class were imprecise and remarkably fluid. Class provided cultural definition and self-identity rather than determining political allegiance. Its value lies in its describing of contemporary attitudes and behaviour rather than its analysis of them. Certainly, the language of class was central to both contemporary writing on Chartism and the analyses of later historians.

In 1854 R. C. Gammage, irritated by his experiences during the later years of the movement, started to publish the first history of the Chartist movement.[5] A revised edition appeared in 1894, some six years after Gammage's death, including some corrections and observations from others in the movement. Gammage's account was regarded rather uncritically as an objective account until, in the early 1950s, John Saville pointed to distortions in his work on the Chartist leader Ernest Jones. In reality, Gammage's book is both a partisan contribution to the movement and a reflection on Chartism.

Gammage stressed the political nature of the movement, an emphasis that is found in many of the large number of contemporary accounts that have survived. The main issue was the vote. However, an alternative view of Chartism was stressed at the time in many middle-class novels on the subject and was put forward dogmatically by Thomas Carlyle in his 1839 pamphlet, *Chartism*. Chartism, he argued, was motivated not by demands for political reform but by the need to improve social conditions. Chartism was, in Carlyle's analysis, the result of 'an abdication on the part of the governors', a breakdown in relations between the classes and a destruction of the 'bond of connection' between the poor and their social 'betters'. What was needed was genuine social under-standing and justice. Four years later, in 'Past and present', Carlyle restated the point:

> We have more riches than any Nation ever had before; we have less good of them than any Nation ever had before. Our successful industry is hitherto unsuccessful; a strange success, if we stop here! In the midst of plethoric plenty, the people perish; with gold walls and full barns, no man feels himself safe or satisfied.[6]

This 'condition-of-England' question influenced such novelists as Charles Dickens, Elizabeth Gaskell and Charles Kingsley, who largely accepted Carlyle's interpretation. Gaskell, in *Mary Barton*, and Kingsley, in *Alton Locke*, created sympathetic Chartist characters, which led many readers – some Chartists but most not – to consider the authors as being receptive to the movement. This is to misread their novels. Neither author had any real warmth for either the Chartist leaders or their political ambitions. *Mary Barton* aroused the sensitivities of Gaskell's novel-reading, middle-class audience by combining sentiment with naturalism and hard facts with deathbed tears. Published in 1848, it seemed to touch the right nerve at the right time. Charles Kingsley's *Alton Locke* (published in 1850) is the story of a young working man who is led by his experience of poverty and distress into following certain immoral and dishonest Chartist leaders who are pursuing political answers to what are moral questions. Kingsley's vivid reconstruction of the Kennington Common 'fiasco' of 10 April 1848 established a negative picture – which was accepted by historians later in the century – of Feargus O'Connor as an ineffective leader and of the whole movement's collapse into chaos and dejection. Spencer Walpole, writing later of 1848, decided that the discovery of fraudulent signatures on the National Petition 'had turned the whole thing into ridicule . . . [and that] the cause of Reform was for years arrested by the abuse of the machinery devised by the Reformers'.[7]

The growth of labour history, 1880–1940

By the 1880s, most British historians had made a link between the political and social interpretations of Chartism. This approach fitted well with the dominant 'Whig' interpretation of history.[8] The Chartist autobiographies published between the 1870s and 1900 with their emphasis on 'respectability' did much to invent the tradition of Chartism as a forerunner of Victorian liberalism. The debate between the old Chartists and the early labour historians was over what Chartism had become. Did the radical Chartist tradition continue into the second half of the century? Had it evolved into socialism, or was Gladstonian liberalism its logical beneficiary?

The confidence of the mid-Victorian economy was undermined by growing foreign competition from the mid-1870s, and the increasing awareness of the extreme poverty that existed in Britain's cities led to a shift in emphasis in the writings on Chartism. The struggling British labour movement moreover became susceptible to charges that socialism was a doctrine of disorder imported from the continent. The result was the development of two major schools of thought – Fabian and Marxist – both of which looked to Chartism for their intellectual origins. The Fabians emerged in the 1880s as a radical 'think-tank' committed to an interventionist solution to the economic and social problems facing society. By contrast, Marxists sought a revolutionary change in society by shifting all the means of economic production, distribution and exchange to democratic government, by establishing working-class power and by recognising the common interests shared by workers across the world. The two approaches may have overlapped, but also led to significantly different perspectives on the history of Chartism. In Beatrice and Sidney Webb's *History of trade unionism* (1894) and Graham Wallas' *The life of Francis Place* (1898), Chartism was accorded a place of some importance – for the Fabians emphasised a radical artisan tradition. By contrast, the Marxists, and especially Marx himself, marginalised the role of artisans within the proletariat. The preoccupation of artisans with changing the political rather than the economic system, and their insistence on a political programme that differed little from that of middle-class radicals in the late eighteenth and nineteenth centuries, posed a fundamental dilemma. Were the Chartists irrelevant in the process of changing the capitalist system, or were they in fact the first proletarian political party? The innumerable references to the Chartists in Marx and Engels' writings meant that Marxist historians paid particular attention to the movement, especially to those Chartists who sought revolutionary solutions.

The first scholarly histories of Chartism appeared between 1895 and 1920. From Germany, John Tildersley explained, in 1898, how the social and economic background of the 1830s and 1840s had affected the course of the movement. In 1914 Edouard Dolléans published *Le Chartisme, 1831–1848*, which came to the single, comprehensive conclusion that Chartism was the reaction of the working class against the Industrial Revolution. Two years later, three studies were published by Columbia University: F. F. Rosenblatt, *The Chartist movement in its social and economic aspects*; P. W. Slosson, *The decline of the Chartist movement*; and H. U. Faulkner, *Chartism and the churches*. Two other writers, both of whom died young, worked on general narrative accounts of Chartism, using the Place manuscripts in the British Library – Mark Hovell of Manchester University was killed in 1916 but Professor T. F. Tout completed his work.[9] Hovell largely followed Francis Place's London-centred, artisanal interpretation of events, arguing that the London Working Men's Association (LWMA) sought, through peaceful campaigning, to achieve its political objectives but that Feargus O'Connor wrenched the initiative from its hands; middle-class opinion was, as a result, alienated. Hovell drew a stark contrast between the rational behaviour of William Lovett and the LWMA, on the one hand, and that of the provincial radicals who were motivated by distress rather than reason, on the other. Julius West's work is more extensive than Hovell's, especially in its examination of the later years of the movement that Hovell did not have time to reach. He too focused on the role of the LWMA, comparing its tactics to those used by the Fabians. He was less hostile to O'Connor, but was still inclined to see him as a would-be dictator.

These works made a similar distinction between the rational, 'moral-force' ideas of Lovett and the LWMA and the 'physical' and potentially explosive outlook of O'Connor and the provincial radicals, a position that dominated the concerns of Chartist historiography until well after 1945. This emphasis derived largely from the use of the Place collection and his judgement that provincial radicals were illiterate and impatient and that their leaders were 'wicked and designing men'. This perspective was of particular value in explaining why Chartism failed to achieve its objectives: the movement was destroyed by divisions within the working class – that is, between the more affluent skilled artisans and the less economically secure factory workers and outworkers. This division between what G. D. H. Cole in 1941 respectively called 'rational Chartism' and 'hungry Chartism' is too convenient a solution, however, and reflects the gradualist approach of the Fabians and liberals rather than the historical record. There is, for example, little to support Hovell's argument that sufficient voters might have been persuaded to support a rationally argued case for the Charter had it not been for the violent rhetoric and behaviour of O'Connor and his supporters.

There was a widening gulf between those who advocated gradualism and the supporters of armed revolution in the aftermath of the 1917 revolution in Russia. Marxist writers declared that Chartism was part of a revolutionary tradition rather than a gradualist movement. Two authors – Theodore Rothstein and Reg Groves – are of particular importance in this respect, because they emphasised the 'class' dimension of the movement. Rothstein's *From Chartism to labourism* was published in 1929. It focused on the recognition by some Chartist writers, especially James Bronterre O'Brien and George Julian Harney, that bourgeois institutions (like the existing parliamentary system) needed to be destroyed more comprehensively than later leaders of the labour movement believed they should be. Rothstein, however, had difficulty in reconciling his views with levels of Chartist agitation that were higher amongst artisans and small masters than they were amongst proletarians in the factories. The Marxist perspective was certainly a useful alternative to the 'Whiggish' views of the Fabians (especially their view that Chartism was the forerunner of the twentieth-century labour movement), but the two approaches did agree on one thing: both were highly critical of the role played by Feargus O'Connor. To the Fabians, and especially to Hovell, O'Connor had destroyed Chartism by his insistence on using a violent rhetoric that prevented the peaceful growth of a rational movement that might otherwise have convinced the authorities of the argument for further reform. For the Marxists, and particularly for Reg Groves in his *But we shall rise again* (1938), it was not O'Connor's violence but his lack of revolutionary vision and his opposition to socialism that deprived the movement of its success.

Biographies and local studies, 1940–80

The general history of Chartism began to be fleshed out after 1939 with the development of two new lines of enquiry: biographies and local studies. The publication of David Williams' study of John Frost in 1939 and G. D. H. Cole's *Chartist portraits* in 1941 opened up a new, biographical dimension to Chartism. The publication of *Chartist studies*, edited by Asa Briggs, in 1959, altered the focus from leaders to localities and resulted in the emergence of sociologically based regional and local studies of the Chartist movement in different parts of the British Isles. These studies underlined the diverse nature of the movement and therefore the difficulty of making generalisations about Chartism as a whole. This point was well made by F. C. Mather in 1965:

> Because Chartism was a product of diverse social forces, the movement itself lacked unity. The division in the Chartist ranks of which historians have been most acutely conscious is that between the advocates of rival methods of winning the Charter – moral force and physical force. This distinction has often been made to appear too clear-cut. What existed was not two schools, but a range of opinions which shaded into one another, and individual Chartists often shifted the emphasis of their views so markedly as to give the impression of having changed sides.[10]

The result of these biographical and local studies was a more rounded, although fragmented, picture of the movement. This is evident in Dorothy Thompson's *The Chartists: popular politics in the Industrial Revolution*, published in

1984. It is an analysis rather than a history of Chartism, and provides a multi-dimensional account of its social composition and values.

By the late 1970s, three types of writing about Chartism had clearly emerged – the generally narrative approach, biographical studies and studies of regional and local events – within two historiographical traditions: the broadly Fabian approach and that of Marxist analysis, grounded particularly in the class dimension. These provided a picture of considerable richness and diversity. There were, however, important questions that had still not been resolved satisfactorily. The emergence of local studies, for example, led historians to question how far Chartism was a movement. Mather quoted an American journal which described Chartism as 'a series of responses, not a movement'.[11] The unity of 1839, it suggested, did not endure, so that the history of Chartism 'must contain not one story, but several interwoven stories'. This kaleidoscopic view of Chartism is important in broadening the understanding of what happened in particular areas of Britain, and of the experience of Chartists in those areas: their concerns, their priorities and their particular political, social and economic agendas. It did, however, thereby pose a challenge to those who saw Chartism as a united campaign at the forefront of an emergent labour movement.

Class, politics and language, 1980–96

The debate over the nature of Chartism in terms of class has lasted for decades, and historians seem to be no closer to resolving it. The problem lies with the word 'class' itself. Many historians derive their understanding of class from the Marxist definition: classes acquired their economic definition from the relationship of their members to the means of production. Inherent in this definition is the notion of class struggle between the owners and non-owners of capital. Some studies demonstrate this class dimension: Ivor Wilks' and D. J. V. Jones' studies of the Newport Rising of 1839, published respectively in 1984 and 1985, for example, show south Wales to have been a society that was deeply divided by perceptions of class and the rising as having been driven by strong class feeling. Malcolm Thomis, by contrast, suggests that only a minority of workers became Chartists, that their enthusiasm was short-lived, and that the norm was widespread working-class apathy to the efforts of their would-be political leaders.[12] Harold Perkin sees class conflict as an expression of an 'immature' rather than of a 'mature' class system.[13] The problem that historians face is that while most in the Chartist movement saw themselves as 'working people', many did not fit into the neat Marxist class category. There may have been a unity of interest within the working population but there were also significant conflicts of interest: artisans had little in common with unskilled workers in industrial towns; the aspirations of Scottish Chartists were not the same as those of Manchester or Birmingham. A strong case can be made that these divisions were of greater significance within Chartism than the potentially unifying effects of class. Richard Dennis sums up the present position: 'Evidently the road to class analysis crosses a minefield with a sniper behind every bush . . . it may not be possible to please all the people all of the time.'[14] The traditional focus on class meant that other societal divisions, such as ethnic and gender groupings, were excluded from serious study.

The answer to this perennial problem may lie in looking at how Chartist contemporaries construed 'class', rather than in relying on later, often politically motivated, definitions. During the 1830s and 1840s, 'class' was a far cruder and flexible concept, used in different ways on different occasions. The underlying effect of the Marxist interpretation of class has been to impose a homogeneity upon the members of the working class, as well as on their class-consciousness, that does not correspond to contemporary experience.

The publication of *The Chartist experience: studies in working class radicalism and culture, 1830–1860*, a collection of essays edited by James Epstein and Dorothy Thompson, marked an important stage in the historiography of Chartism. It contained the paper by Gareth Stedman Jones entitled 'The language of Chartism', which he republished in extended form the following year; this reasserted the centrality of politics in the Chartist agitation. He argued that Chartism inherited from earlier radical movements not only their essentially political programme of the mass platform but also their analyses of oppression and distress. He suggests that there was little hostility between employees and capitalists as such, and that the basic causes of exploitation were seen as being political rather than economic. The crucial dividing line between the classes was not determined by their respective economic roles but by the division established by the 1832 Reform Act between those who possessed political power and those who were denied it. Chartism, in this analysis, was a populist political movement of 'the people', rather than an economic 'class' movement. The 'class' argument, it appears, has fallen from favour. Revisionist historians have become increasingly suspicious of the priority that previous historians of Chartism gave to social and economic considerations. New political and cultural agendas are now being explored.[15]

One of the main reasons for this process of revision has been the recent reappraisal of the concept of the 'Industrial Revolution'. Historians are increasingly recognising the fact that urban artisans, rural domestic workers and factory operatives co-existed within a complex and fluid economic structure, and that the move towards factory production was cautious and far from complete by the late 1830s. There was little common national experience among workers, and, however much they may attract historians, appeals to working-class unity at anything more than the level of particular communities were not a major facet of contemporary experience. Such a diverse and pluralistic nature of social identity and relationships has led some post-structuralist historians to focus on the 'representational': the construction of identity and social reality through language and discourse. This post-modern approach regards the ways in which language is used, rather than class, as a means of uniting workers whose surrounding physical conditions and experience of industrialisation significantly differed.[16]

The cultural approach to Chartism is important. Indeed, historians have identified a 'Chartist culture': there were networks of schools, discussion groups, libraries, churches and other meeting places where politics could be debated and views shared. These served to inform, if not to define, the development and reception of the Chartist programme during the 1830s and 1840s. Radical rhetoric was language in action, a cultural expression of deep-seated political, economic and social grievances. It was vibrant, highly ritualised, grounded in the streets as much as in the discussion halls, and essentially oral. Reading the 'texts', as post-structural historians would have us do, reinforces notions of the continuity of radical action across the nineteenth century and neglects the dynamism and unpredictability of the movement. Although the Charter may have provided a unifying programme, locally and nationally the debate was a confused combination of rhetoric, organisation, agitation, constitutional culture, rituals, symbols, iconography and personalities. The Chartists may have found it difficult to establish a distinct identity but those historians who write Chartism off as simply a failure have not recognised the feelings, perceptions and aspirations of working people of the 1830s and 1840s and, arguably, also those of today.

Notes and references

1 J. F. C. Harrison, *The common people*, London, 1984, p. 261.

2 Useful summaries of the historiography of Chartism can be found in Dorothy Thompson, 'Chartism and the historians', in *Outsiders: class, gender and nation*, London, 1993, pp. 19–44; Miles Taylor, 'Rethinking the Chartists: searching for synthesis in the historiography of Chartism', *Historical Journal*, vol. 39 (1996); and John Charlton, *The Chartists: the first national workers' movement*, London, 1997, pp. 90–95.

3 The literature on Marx and Engels is immense. Of particular importance in understanding how they viewed industrial and urban society are F. Engels, *The condition of the working class in England in 1844*, Leipzig, 1845; K. Marx and F. Engels, *The Communist manifesto*, 1848, London, 1850; and K. Marx, *Capital*, vol. 1, London, 1867. See also Charlton, *The Chartists*, pp. 87–89, for a brief discussion of Marx and Engels on Chartism.

4 Benjamin Disraeli, *Sybil or the two nations*, London, 1845. See also the discussion of Disraeli as 'industrial' novelist in Raymond Williams, *Culture and society, 1780–1950*, London, 1958 (Penguin edn, 1963, pp. 99–119). Louis Cazamian, *The social novel in England, 1830–1850*, Paris, 1903 (first published in translation in London, 1973) is still, despite its age, perhaps the clearest discussion of the genre.

5 R. C. Gammage, *The history of the Chartist movement, from its commencement down to the present times*, 1st edn, London, 1855, 2nd edn, Newcastle, 1894, reprinted 1969. A useful discussion of Gammage and his *History*, especially the differences between the two editions, can be found in Joyce M. Bellamy and John Saville (eds.), *Dictionary of labour history*, vol. 6, London, 1982, and in Saville's introduction to the 1969 reprint.

6 'Past and Present', printed in Alan Shelston (ed.), *Thomas Carlyle: selected writings*, London, 1971, p. 263.

7 Quoted in J. T. Ward, *Chartism*, London, 1973, p. 7.

8 On the historiographical framework for the development of labour history, see Christopher Parker, *The English historical tradition since 1850*, Edinburgh, 1990.

9 Mark Hovell, *The Chartist movement*, Manchester, 1918.

10 F. C. Mather, *Chartism*, London, 1965, p. 15.

11 *Victorian Studies*, vol. 5.3 (1962), p. 266.

12 Malcolm I. Thomis, *Responses to industrialisation: the British experience, 1780–1850*, Newton Abbot, 1976, and M. I. Thomis and Peter Holt, *Threats of revolution in Britain, 1789–1848*, London, 1977, pp. 100–16, contain the best summary of Thomis' position.

13 Harold Perkin, *The origins of modern English society, 1780–1880*, London, 1969, especially chapters 6 and 7.

14 Richard Dennis, *English industrial cities of the nineteenth century*, Cambridge, 1984, pp. 184–85.

15 John Belchem, 'Beyond Chartist studies: class, community and party in early Victorian popular politics', in Derek Fraser (ed.), *Cities, class and communication: essays in honour of Asa Briggs*, Hemel Hempstead, 1990, is a useful summary of some of the debates of the 1980s. Neville Kirk, 'Setting the standard: Dorothy Thompson, the discipline of historical context and the study of Chartism', in Owen Ashton *et al.* (eds.), *The duty of discontent: essays for Dorothy Thompson*, 1996, is invaluable for following up these debates, as well as providing a vital analysis of a seminal figure in the development of how historians view Chartism.

16 The post-modern approach is best explored in Patrick Joyce, *Visions of the people: industrial England and the question of class, 1840–1914*, Cambridge, 1991; Patrick Joyce, *Democratic subjects*, Cambridge, 1994; James Vernon, *Politics and the people: a study in English political culture, 1815–1867*, Cambridge, 1993; and James Vernon (ed.), *Re-reading the constitution: new narratives in the political history of England's long nineteenth century*, Cambridge, 1996. At a theoretical level, see Alan Munslow, *Deconstructing history*, London, 1997, and the papers in Keith Jenkins (ed.), *The postmodern history reader*, London, 1997. Richard J. Evans, *In defence of history*, London, 1997, is a blistering attack on all things post-modern.

The emergence of Chartism

Radical politics during the 1830s was a confused and confusing jumble: it lacked cohesion and had little unity. If it is possible to identify its one overwhelming characteristic, it was fluidity. Radicals moved freely from one agitation to another: from campaigning for an unstamped press, to supporting the Tolpuddle Martyrs, to resisting the 1834 Poor Law Amendment Act. Economic demands merged into calls for political reform and for a fairer society.

Chartism first appeared in the spring of 1838 with the publication of the People's Charter. This document was produced following consultation between such leading radical MPs as John Arthur Roebuck and representatives of the LWMA, which had been established in 1836 to campaign for 'an equality of political rights'. The implementation of the 'six points' of the Charter – universal manhood suffrage, vote by secret ballot instead of public voting on the hustings, the abolition of property qualifications for MPs, payment of MPs, equal electoral districts of constituencies of roughly equal size, and annual parliaments – were considered necessary to secure this equality.

A 'mass platform'

The 'mass platform' was central to working-class radicalism during the first half of the nineteenth century. The key figure in its promotion was Henry 'Orator' Hunt. Under his leadership, between 1815 and the passage of the Reform Act in 1832, this popular movement developed a political discourse and programme that defined its beliefs and analysis, as well as its tactics and class interests, all of which remained largely unchallenged until the final breakdown of Chartism during the late 1840s.[1] Hunt argued that radicals must maintain the interests of the hard-working sections of society against the grasping plunderers that were representative of the 'Old Corruption'. What separated the rich from the poor, he believed, was an aristocratic monopoly over effective political power. So what was needed was a constitutional solution through parliamentary reform and a redistribution of power. This political analysis was simple to understand and quickly came to dominate radical discourse; economic distress was thereby politicised. Hunt's was an eminently practical ideology, which lacked the abstract, philosophical language of the theory of natural rights put forward by writers like Thomas Paine in his *Rights of man* in the 1790s, and was grounded in the brutal realities of life for most working people.

Hunt's message was also constitutional. He was determined that there should be no compromise with any parliamentary allies and no dilution of the

Britons strike home by the contemporary cartoonist, George Cruickshank, shows his view of the Peterloo Massacre of 16 August 1819, when 11 people were killed and hundreds injured. A peaceful crowd of 60,000 men, women and children were brutally dispersed by mounted yeomanry at St Peter's Field in Manchester, where they had gathered to hear Henry 'Orator' Hunt demand government reform. Establishment fear of violent revolution from below was a recurrent theme throughout the nineteenth century.

demanded principles of universal suffrage, annual parliaments and the secret ballot. Hunt's was an open, unconspiratorial message. In John Belchem's words, it was a 'strategy of intimidation, an escalating policy of open agitation which drew on the rich rhetoric of "people's history", celebrating the glorious struggle against absolutism and the ultimate constitutional right of physical resistance'.[2] The constitutional nature of the mass platform was distorted by later writers. It was dismissed by Marxist historians as a diversion from the development of a revolutionary solution, while Whig historians presented it as a sign of the innate 'respectability' of the working-class demands for reform. The advantage of this constitutional position, and something that the Chartists inherited, was that the radicals could paint themselves as the defenders of constitutional freedom and the rule of law. This was a disciplined form of mass extra-parliamentary protest, its force essentially moral and its violence rhetorical. It sought legitimacy through the power of public opinion and dispassionate justice. Such a position did not rule out the use of physical violence, but Hunt and later radicals argued that this should only be used when in a position of strength, when no one could doubt its morality or validity.

The focus on legitimacy was politically naive. The events following the Peterloo Massacre demonstrate the difficulty faced by radicals, a story replayed on several occasions during the 1830s and 1840s. The actions of the Manchester magistrates on 16 August 1819 in ordering cavalry to disperse a peaceful meeting had given the moral high ground to the radicals: how, many people argued, was it possible to justify the slaughter of innocent men, women and children who were simply pursuing their constitutional right to protest? Constitutional right may have been on Hunt's side, but was this sufficient to justify direct action? While the radicals hesitated, their mass support evaporated and the authorities regained the political initiative. The problem facing Hunt and later Feargus O'Connor was that although the mass platform could produce mass support and mass action, it could not deliver constitutional change. The debate that followed the collapse of the mass platform in late 1819 is redolent of the debates within Chartism during the 1830s and 1840s. If the government was not prepared to concede constitutional change, and if there was limited support for direct physical action, what could the radicals do? William Cobbett, and later the Chartist leader William Lovett, were prepared to be pragmatic, seeking support and reform where they could rather than sticking to the fundamentalist universal-suffrage position. Others, like Richard Carlile during the 1820s and George Julian Harney and Ernest Jones during the late 1840s, turned away from the mass platform in search of alternative ideologies and solutions.

The 'betrayal' of 1832

The origins of Chartism can be traced back to the early 1830s and in particular to the frustration or 'betrayal' that many radicals felt at the conclusion of the reform agitation between 1830 and 1832.[3] This was a period of great political excitement as the Whig government of Earl Grey sought to introduce a measure of parliamentary reform, but in many respects, working-class radicals were bit-players in the whole process. The working-class radical leadership was, however, split over reform. Francis Place and William Cobbett saw the proposed Whig reforms relatively positively: as a stepping stone, an initial breach in the defences of the aristocratic monopoly of power. Henry Hunt, by contrast, uncompromising as ever over the need for universal suffrage, was opposed by much of the London-based radical press and directed his attentions to the working population of the north. Divisions in London, between Place's National Political Union and the more radical National Union of the Working Classes, were paralleled in the provinces. Agitation in Leicester and Birmingham, however, was marked by a degree of collaboration between the moderate, politically conscious working population and the middle classes, but this was unusual and the picture in towns like Manchester and Leeds contrasted sharply with Birmingham and Leicester. The Manchester Political Union, for example, was made up largely of the lower-middle class rather than working people, although it had little sympathy with the industrialists and mill-owners; it was opposed by a working-class political union pledged to universal suffrage. These complex social divisions were reproduced in other northern cities, like Leeds, Bradford and Bolton.

The volatility of working-class support was also of doubtful value to the middle classes. No one with property – from the middle class or the aristocracy – was happy about civil disorder. While the threat of potential disturbance was a valuable lever for reformers, actual violence threatened political suicide, with a rapid loss of 'respectable' support among the working as well as the middle classes. Despite what some historians maintain, a working-class revolution was hardly an option between 1830 and 1832. The famous run on the banks, when Place urged people to withdraw their savings in 'the days of May', never materialised. It was the Whig threat to create new peers, thereby breaking the Tory monopoly in the upper house, that persuaded the Lords to change their minds. Yet these 'ten days of the English revolution' in May 1832 created a popular myth that played a central role in the attitudes and tactics of the Chartists. Many people believed that the Whigs had been carried back into power on the shoulders of the people and that, as a result, reform had been achieved. If it were possible to repeat the strength and vitality of this pressure, radicals believed, then similar results could be accomplished.

Was parliamentary reform the 'great betrayal', as many working-class radicals came to believe? To view 1832 in this way underestimates the degree of support for reform among the working population, as well as demonstrating a misunderstanding of the Whigs' intentions. They never promised to give in to working-class demands for universal suffrage; Hunt was right on that issue. The basic Whig argument, which was repeated frequently, was that reform was necessary to preserve the existing system of government, and that meant attaching the middle classes to the existing constitution by giving them the vote. Failure to do this was rightly recognised as more likely to lead to revolution than working-class agitation would. Conservatism was therefore at the heart of the reforms. The Whigs believed that they could strengthen existing society, and giving the working classes the vote was never part of the political equation. The Whigs may have been successful in attaching the middle classes to the constitution and in maintaining the dominance of landed society – both in politics and society – but they completely failed to achieve their second aim, that of finality. It was the Tories who saw concession as inviting further demands for reform and they therefore believed that finality was an illusion. The Tory apologist Croker wrote: 'the Reform Bill is . . . a stepping stone in England to a Republic . . . the Bill once passed, good night to the Monarchy and the Lords and the Church'.[4] Many working-class radicals rejected the reforms as being too moderate, and even those who had supported it believed that it was merely a step on the road towards universal suffrage. Bronterre O'Brien wrote that reform was 'part payment of the debt of right due to us . . . capable of expanding and purifying itself into a perfect representation system'.[5] The working population was still excluded from parliament. The mass platform was again in tatters.

The attitude of the Whigs

Chartism emerged as a political movement as a result of the attitude of the Whig government which adopted policies that were seen by many working people as being contrary to their interests.[6] They increasingly felt that they had been duped by the middle classes. The Whig policies were, in many respects, an extension of reforms begun in the 1820s; but this was not the 1820s and, far from stabilising and rationalising government, reform in 1832 had instead raised popular expectations.

The anti-stamp legislation

The Whigs took an uncompromising position with regard to working-class movements. Between 1830 and 1836 they waged a relentless war against the unstamped radical press.[7] A stamp duty had been placed on newspapers in the eighteenth century. This pushed up their cost and, people believed, would thus keep them out of the hands of the working classes. Both working- and middle-class reformers opposed the 'taxes on knowledge' imposed after 1830. Individuals like Henry Hetherington and John Cleave were involved in a determined effort to break the press laws by publishing and distributing hundreds of illegal tracts and newspapers; over 700 sellers of radical journals were prosecuted. Government repression proved largely unsuccessful, however, and in March 1836 the newspaper duty was reduced to a penny, thus effectively ending the agitation. This was a compromise that satisfied much middle-class opinion but that left sections of the working class nursing a similar sense of betrayal to that of 1832.

The anti-stamp agitation played an important role in the development of radicalism during the 1830s. The LWMA, for example, was formed in 1836 by William Lovett after the Association of Working Men to Procure a Cheap and Honest Press, which had co-ordinated the agitation, was disbanded. It also demonstrated the ideological divisions within working-class radicalism. Two rhetorics prevailed in the unstamped press. The older position attacked the whole structure of the 'Old Corruption', focusing its attacks on taxes, rents, pensions, the aristocracy and the established church. The newer, 'class' position, which viewed the middle class with suspicion, was based on a more sophisticated analysis of industrial society, and was grounded in a critique of property, power and exploitation. Patricia Hollis rightly argues that historians should not overestimate the division within radical opinion. Indeed, there were more than two radical publics clamouring for a hearing, for much as the Chartists could agree on the necessity for the Charter, so radicals of all classes believed that a free press and a wider suffrage were inseparable. How they reached that standpoint varied.

Trade-union activity

Trade-union activity was a further avenue for the expression of organised working-class pressure. The Combination Acts had banned unions between 1799 and 1824.[8] These were both unpopular among the skilled workers who made up the majority of trade unionists and extremely ineffective. They limited rather than crushed the growth of union activity. Their repeal in 1824 was quickly followed by legislation in 1825 that gave unions a certain legal status but effectively denied them the right to strike by restoring the criminal law of conspiracy. The explosion of trade-union activity between 1829 and 1834, when attempts were made to set up general unions of skilled workers and to adopt radical social and economic theories, concerned the government. John Doherty, for example, attempted to establish a general union of cotton-spinners for England, Scotland and Wales, and later the National Association for the Protection of Labour, while in 1834 Robert Owen played an important role in the development of the Grand National Consolidated Trades Union (GNCTU). Employers were hostile, however, and most of the skilled trade unionists outside London stood aloof; it was the traditional 'knife-and-fork' issues of wages, working hours and conditions that concerned them, rather than any abstract, radical theories.

All these attempts at establishing general unions collapsed. The Whig attitude towards trade unions was ambiguous. Lord Melbourne, as home secretary, encouraged local magistrates to use all the legal powers available to smash what he regarded as such violent and criminal combinations, scandalously giving considerable guidance and assistance to magistrates in the case of the Tolpuddle Martyrs, six agricultural workers from Tolpuddle in Dorset who were convicted of administering an illegal oath and condemned to transportation to Australia. His actions were widely deplored outside parliament, and on 21 April 1834 a procession of at least 30,000 radicals and trade unionists marched through the streets of London in protest at the sentences. Lord John Russell, however, differed from Melbourne as to the gravity of their crime and, when he replaced Melbourne at the Home Office in 1835, pardoned the six labourers.

After the excitement generated by the GNCTU and the Tolpuddle Martyrs it was, as one historian has said, 'business as usual' for many in the trade-union movement. Its growth continued, despite the trade depression that developed after 1836, especially among iron-workers and engineers. As the 1830s progressed, many trade unionists came to attribute their various defeats to a single cause: the reformed parliament which had denied them the right of combination. The arrest and prosecution of members of the Glasgow cotton-spinners' union in July 1837 on suspicion of arson and murder led to a widespread campaign in their support throughout Scotland and northern England. This campaign, as well as the general struggle to defend union rights, carried many workers into Chartism.

Factory reform

That the reformed parliament failed to provide any real improvement in factory conditions became an additional source of political discontent.[9] The Ten Hour movement, which agitated for a reduction in working hours, and which had its origins in Yorkshire in late 1830, was but one expression of this dissatisfaction. The demand for factory reform split the main political groupings and economic interests: Tories, Whigs and radicals were divided on the issue, as were agrarian and industrial representatives. The campaign, which took place at the same time as the reform agitation, was based in the textile districts of England and Scotland, was organised by Richard Oastler and was financed by wealthy Tory Anglican manufacturers like John Fielden of Todmorden and William Walker of Bradford.

The alliance between such Tory Anglicans and working-class radicals in the early 1830s to improve conditions in the burgeoning cotton and woollen mills of the north may, in retrospect, seem strange. For Tory Anglicans it was a matter of humanitarian concern, a reassertion of their belief in the centrality of pater-nalism to a stable, ordered society. For working-class radicals it was a case of improving working conditions and reducing exploitation – justice and fairness in the workplace. Yet these working-class radicals were prepared to ignore the conservative attitudes of many Tory Anglicans to parliament or the established church and their opposition to parliamentary reform. For them it was a matter of priorities. Indeed, there was no inconsistency in workers' eyes between their support for factory, as well as political, reform, especially since it was the nonconformist liberal manufacturers (who supported parliamentary reform but opposed universal suffrage) who were seen as the main exploiters of factory labour. In the event, the Whig government effectively hijacked the movement and, although it regulated the working day of children in the textile industry, the government-sponsored 1833 Factory Act left adults' hours unaltered. The movement never regained its momentum after 1834, and many of its leaders became involved in the anti-Poor Law agitation. The frustrated factory reformers swelled the rising Chartist tide and many of the northern delegates of the Chartist Convention in 1839 had initially entered politics through the Ten Hour movement.

Poor Law reform

Many had also gained their political experience through their involvement in the campaign against the imposition of the new Poor Law, arguably the least popular of all Whig measures.[10] Demands for reform of the Poor Law surfaced after 1815; the Poor Law, contemporaries argued, placed an unacceptably heavy burden on property owners, especially in rural areas. It was regarded as being ineffective, and some believed that it encouraged working people to have large families. The Whigs established a Royal Commission to investigate the issue in 1832 and it reported its findings in 1834. Dominated by orthodox political economists like Nassau Senior and Benthamites like Edwin Chadwick, it sought to expunge the abuses of the old system and to replace it with a more punitive and clearly deterrent system of poor relief. Poverty, the commission argued, was the result of individual moral failings and needed to be tackled in a less sympathetic manner than under the old system.

The 1834 Poor Law Amendment Act largely implemented the recommendations of the commission. It grouped parishes – the unit of administration established under the old Poor Law – into Poor Law unions governed by elected boards of guardians. It also reduced the cost of relief by introducing a stringent workhouse test: the poor could no longer receive outdoor relief (a form of benefit) in their own homes; if they wanted relief, it had to be within the workhouse. To ensure that the new system was applied in a uniform manner, a central board of three Poor Law commissioners, assisted by assistant commissioners, laid down national standards.

Although the 1834 Act met little opposition in parliament, a widespread and vociferous protest campaign quickly developed, first in rural, and then in industrial, England. The campaign against the act in southern and eastern England was intense but fruitless. There were no leaders operating at more than a local level and there was little real attempt to co-ordinate the actions of the scattered rural population. Things were very different in the north, where the act was bitterly resisted. Here the workhouses became the symbol of Whig cruelty, the 'Bastilles' of the 1830s. Opposition became obvious in late 1836, when the commissioners began to introduce the new Poor Law north of the Trent and the committees of the factory movement were transformed into anti-Poor Law organisations in response. Richard Oastler led the attack, but Feargus O'Connor, Joseph Rayner Stephens, and London-based radicals like Henry Hetherington and James Bronterre O'Brien soon joined him. The commissioners misunderstood the nature of poverty in the industrial north, assuming that it was the same as that in the south and east. It was not: for most industrial workers, poor relief was viewed not as an essential means of subsistence but as financial support when they were suddenly thrown out of work because of a downturn in trade. For them, as well as the local magistrates and Poor Law officials, the old system had worked effectively, and they strongly objected to interference from London in their local affairs. Furthermore, the timing of the act's introduction was, to say the least, unfortunate, coinciding as it did with the beginning of the intense trade depression that lasted until the early 1840s. The circulation of exaggerated stories of starvation and ill-treatment in the new workhouses further inflamed passions.

The anti-Poor Law campaign in northern England proved very successful: outbreaks of violence, awkward local officials, the inability of the central commissioners to insist on the enforcement of the new system – all conspired to dilute the process of implementation. Thus no workhouse was built in the West Riding until the 1840s and the workhouse test was never effectively enforced. Between 1838 and 1839 the campaign was beginning to run out of steam, but by then it had already done significant damage.

The new Poor Law was regarded by the radicals as yet another example of Whig betrayal, of government not on behalf of the people but for, as Bronterre O'Brien wrote in early 1837, 'the monied or property owning classes'. Gradually the north turned to a wider-based radicalism, and O'Connor revived the mass platform.

An economic imperative

Growing economic depression was increasing the discontentment. Poor harvests resulted in heavy grain imports, especially in 1838 and 1839, which did little to reduce the high price of food and depressed home demand. Disillusionment with foreign borrowers in the United States and elsewhere discouraged investment abroad, thereby reducing British exports. Prices had begun to fall in the cotton industry as early as 1833, when signs of over-production first became obvious. Mill-owners, who were committed to costly plant and equipment, could not afford to limit their output in order to keep prices up and initially capacity actually increased. By 1837, however, the cotton industry was depressed, not seriously at first, but conditions gradually worsened, particularly when between 1841 and 1842 mill-owners in Belgium, Saxony and Prussia – heavy buyers of British yarn – reduced their consumption. British producers pumped more and more goods into foreign markets in an effort to restore their earnings, with catastrophic effects on cotton prices.

Similar trends were evident in other industries: by 1842 the wool trade was in deep depression, while the coal and iron industries also faced problems. Increased demand for coal during the early 1830s and correspondingly rising coal prices had stimulated capital investment. This too led to over-production: between 1836 and 1843 coal output rose by between 60 and 70 per cent, while demand increased by only 30 per cent. Attempts by colliery owners to control output using quotas failed, however, and the industry slumped. The iron industry followed a parallel pattern: output had grown in south Wales and Staffordshire (but most dramatically in Scotland), but by 1840 the industry was becoming increasingly unprofitable, mainly due to the fact that the speculative boom in railways and shipbuilding – a major source of employment after 1836 – was largely exhausted by 1840.

The problem faced by the manufacturing economy of the late 1830s was therefore largely one of over-production, which home and export markets were unable to absorb. The interconnected nature of the economy reinforced this depressed state: coal depended on iron, iron on demand for industrial expansion at home and abroad, while demand depended both on an ability and a willingness to invest, as well as upon earnings. Depression in one area thus impacted on others. Britain's trading policy did not help this situation. As the price of Britain's exports fell faster than those of imports, so the relative cost of imported raw materials and food increased. Between 1836 and 1840 the value of imports stood at over £5 million a year more than exports. By 1840 tariffs on imports made up nearly half of the nation's total revenue. Far from protecting the British economy against foreign competition, this tariff policy pushed up production costs and, as a result, employers sought to reduce their labour costs by cutting wages and laying off workers. The outcome was rising levels of unemployment and widespread 'distress'. The 'politics of hunger' played a significant role in the emergence of Chartism.

Conclusions

The passage of measures of reform in 1832 had heightened expectations among the working and, to a lesser extent the middle, classes that the Whigs were either unwilling or unable to meet. It was no coincidence that Chartism and the Anti-Corn Law League both emerged between 1838 and 1839. Towards the end of the decade, increasing anger over Whig attitudes towards the press and trade unionism, the frustrations of factory reformers and the fear generated by the new Poor Law, as well as the effects of trade depression, boiled over into general demands for further political reform. The agitators believed that this was the only means of remedying the specific grievances of the working population and of maintaining or improving their material living standards. Yet to see Chartism simply as a 'knife-and-fork' issue is to misunderstand the profound political loathing with which the Whigs were regarded.

The LWMA was one of several organisations created during the course of the late 1830s that expressed working-class frustration, disappointment and disillusionment. The East London Democratic Association, founded in early 1837, and Feargus O'Connor's and his Irish supporters' Marylebone Radical Association, although more militant, had similar objectives to the LWMA. In May 1837, Thomas Attwood's Birmingham Political Union, which had been stagnant since 1832, was revived, and further political unions sprang up in other places like Manchester. The key figure in channelling these separate grievances into a general demand for parliamentary reform was Feargus O'Connor. He founded his own organisation – the Great Northern Union – in 1838, and was able to win substantial support from the Birmingham Political Union and the LWMA. The winter of 1838 to 1839 was spent by many radicals preparing for the forthcoming Chartist Convention and the subsequent presentation of the Charter to parliament. It is, however, important not to exaggerate the organic unity of Chartism. The unity that existed was fuelled by a pervasive sense of resentment, but at all levels of the movement different emphases, tactics and organisations gave Chartism its 'kaleidoscopic appearance'.

What was behind the emergence of Chartism?

1.1 Political solutions

Your petitioners dwell in a land whose merchants are noted for enterprise, whose manufacturers are very skilful and where workmen are proverbial for industry. The land itself is goodly, the soil is rich, the temperature wholesome . . . Yet with all these elements of natural prosperity and with every disposition and capacity to take advantage of them we find ourselves overwhelmed with public and private starving . . . Our traders are trembling on the verge of bankruptcy; our workmen are starving; capital brings no profit and labour no renumeration, the home of the artificer is desolate and the warehouse of the pawnbroker is full . . . The good of the party has been advanced to sacrifice the good of the nation . . . It was the expectation of the people that a remedy for the greater part if not the whole of their grievances would be found in the Reform Act of 1832 . . . They have been bitterly and basely deceived.

Source: from the Chartist Petition, 1839

1.2 The 'condition-of-England' question

Chartism means the bitter discontent grown fierce and made, the wrong condition therefore or the wrong disposition of the Working Classes of England . . . The matter of Chartism did not begin yesterday; will by no means end this day or tomorrow. Reform Ministry, constabulary rural police, new levy of soldiers, grants of money to Birmingham . . . all this will put down only the embodiment . . . of Chartism . . . The melancholy fact remains, that this thing known at present by the name of Chartism does exist; has existed, and, either put down, into secret treason, with rusty pistols, vitriol-bottle and match-box, or openly brandishing pike and torch (one knows not in which case more fatal-looking), is like to exist till quite other methods have been tried with it . . . Delirious Chartism will not have raged to no purpose . . . if it has forced all thinking men of the community to think of this vital matter . . . Is the condition of the English working people wrong; so wrong that rational working men cannot, will not, and even should not rest quiet under it?

Source: Thomas Carlyle, 'Chartism', 1839, printed in Alan Shelston (ed.), *Thomas Carlyle: selected writings*, London, 1971, pp. 151–53

1.3 The social question

Political reforms were certainly valued because of their abstract justice, but they were also looked upon as a means of securing a better social position for the humbler classes . . . It may be doubted whether there was ever a great political movement of the people without a social origin. The chief material object of mankind is to possess the means of social enjoyment. Secure them in possession of these and small is the care they have for political abstractions. It is the existence of great social wrongs which principally teaches the masses the value of political rights . . . let that prosperity be succeeded by a period of adversity and the waves of popular discontent will roll with such impetuous force as to threaten the safety of the political fabric. The masses look on the enfranchised classes, whom they behold reposing on the couch of opulence, and contrast that opulence with the misery of their own condition. Reasoning from effect to cause there is no marvel that they arrive at the conclusion – that their exclusion from political power is the cause of our social anomalies. There might be no clear idea in their minds at the commencement of the movement for the Charter of the way in which political power was worked to their disadvantage. Still less might they be aware of the nature of those social measures which the possession of that power would enable them to apply for the improvement of their condition.

Source: R. C. Gammage, *The history of the Chartist movement, from its commencement down to present times, 1837–1854*, Newcastle, 1894, reprinted 1969, p. 9

1.4 Resolving the contradictions?

Contemporaries noted that for many of its followers Chartism was basically 'a knife and fork question'. Yet its programme was a series of political demands. This has puzzled historians, who have concluded that one of the main reasons for Chartism's lack of success was its contradiction in seeking political remedies for economic grievances. In fact the Chartists' tactics made a good deal of sense at that time, and their analysis of what we should now call the power structure was evidently shrewder than the historians'. The link between economic ills and political representation was constantly elaborated in Chartist pamphlets and oratory; how, it was asked, could a 'rotten House of Commons', representing the interests of landowners, speculators, manufacturers and capitalists, be expected to do anything but uphold an economic system in which the poor were ground down and oppressed?

Source: J. F. C. Harrison, *The common people*, London, 1984, p. 261

Document case-study questions

1 How do the writers of 1.1 account for the state of the country that they describe?

2 How far do the authors of 1.1 and 1.2 agree in their view of the situation that had produced Chartism?

3 In what respects does 1.3 give a valid explanation for the development of Chartism?

4 '1.1, 1.2 and 1.3 give contradictory explanations for the emergence of Chartism during the late 1830s.' Do you agree with this statement and, if so, why?

5 1.1 and 1.2 provide contemporary accounts of Chartism, while 1.3 was written later. Do you think that 1.3 provides a better account and, if so, why?

6 'Economic conditions stimulated political responses; 1.4 allows historians to resolve the thorny question of the causation of Chartism.' Discuss.

7 Was Chartism the result of frustrated expectation? Explain your answer.

Notes and references

1 The development of the 'mass platform' can be best approached in John Belchem, *'Orator' Hunt: Henry Hunt and English working-class radicalism*, Oxford, 1985.

2 Belchem, *'Orator' Hunt*, p. 4.

3 M. Brock, *The Great Reform Act*, London, 1973 is the standard text, while E. J. Evans, *The Great Reform Act of 1832*, 2nd edn, London, 1995, is a shorter starting point. Two books by Norman Gash, *Politics in the age of Peel*, Brighton, 2nd edn, 1978, and *Reaction and reconstruction in English politics, 1832–1852*, Oxford, 1965, provide the best analyses of the operation of the electoral system after 1832.

4 L. J. Jennings (ed.), *Correspondence and diaries of J. W. Croker*, vol. 2, London, 1884, pp. 140, 148.

5 *Midland Representative*, 18 February 1832.

6 On the 1830s and the Whigs in general, see Geoffrey Finlayson, *England in the 1830s*, London, 1969. Ian Newbould, *Whiggery and reform, 1830–41: the politics of government*, London, 1990, and Peter Mandler, *Aristocratic government in the age of reform*, Oxford, 1990, are useful for a discussion of Whig reforms.

7 P. Hollis, *The pauper press: a study in working-class radicalism of the 1830s*, Oxford, 1970, W. H. Wickwar, *The struggle for the freedom of the press, 1819–1832*, London, 1928, and J. Wiener, *The war of the unstamped*, Ithaca, 1969, are essential reading on the agitation to abolish newspaper taxes.

8 H. Pelling, *A history of British trade unionism*, London, 1993, and A. E. Musson, *British trade unions, 1800–1875*, London, 1972, provide useful background. J. Rule (ed.), *British trade unionism, 1750–1850: the formative years*, London, 1988, is a valuable collection of papers.

9 The shortest introduction to the factory-reform movement is Ursula Henriques, *The early Factory Acts and their enforcement*, London, 1971. J. T. Ward, *The factory movement, 1830–1850*, London, 1962, is the most detailed study, but must now be supplemented, and in some areas superseded, by Robert Gray, *The factory question and industrial England, 1830–1860*, Cambridge, 1996.

10 A. Brundage, *The making of the new Poor Law, 1833–39*, London, 1979, A. Digby, *The Poor Law in nineteenth-century England and Wales*, London, 1982, D. Fraser (ed.), *The new Poor Law in the nineteenth century*, London, 1976, and M. E. Rose, *The relief of poverty, 1834–1914*, 2nd edn, London, 1985, are the most useful books on the introduction and operation of the new Poor Law. Details of the opposition to the 1834 Act can be found in N. Edsall, *The anti-Poor Law movement, 1833–1844*, Manchester, 1971, and J. Knott, *Popular opposition to the 1834 Poor Law*, London, 1985.

Who were the Chartists?

In late 1851, an article entitled 'How I became a rebel' was published in the *Christian Socialist*.[1] The author of this incomplete autobiography was an anonymous former Chartist. Although it may be unclear whether his narrative is about 1839 or 1848, he left little doubt about his reasons for becoming a Chartist:

> And so, Lord John [Russell], I became a Rebel: – that is to say: – Hungry in a land of plenty, I began seriously to question for the first time in my life to enquire WHY, WHY – a dangerous question, Lord John, isn't it, for a poor man to ask? Leading to anarchy and confusion . . . Politics, my Lord, was with me then, a bread-and-cheese question. Let me not, however, be mistaken; – I ever loved the idea of freedom – glorious freedom, and its inevitable consequences – and not only for what it will fetch, but the *holy principle*.

This source makes explicit that the reason why some people became Chartists was a combination of principle and pragmatism. 'Want' may have been the spur to action, but behind the harsh realities of poverty, unemployment and depression lay an important belief in freedom and justice. The Charter, its proponents believed, was the means through which a 'just' society could be established, a society in which the economic problems that afflicted working people could be abolished.

Some general observations

Chartism was different from earlier radical movements. It had objectives that were shared by all its supporters, even if they differed on how those objectives were to be achieved. Its support came from across the country. It was principally a working-class movement. It lasted longer. The Chartists of 1838–39 did not correspond to those of 1842 and 1848. At different times, for different reasons and in different parts of the country, different types of working people found in the Charter a means of improving their lives. This helps to explain why it is difficult to answer the question 'Who were the Chartists?' It is important to recognise that, while it is necessary to make some general statements about the nature of Chartist support, it is at the local level that historians must search to find convincing explanations for it.[2]

A geographical dimension

The real power base of Chartism lay in the three textile districts of the East Midlands, the West Riding of Yorkshire and in southern Lancashire. Within these areas, Chartism was stronger in industrial villages and medium-sized towns like Stockport and Bradford than in the major provincial centres of Manchester and Leeds. But there were other areas involved, like south Wales, the Black Country and parts of the south-west, where there had been little organised radicalism before. In the first National Petition, 19,000 signatures came from London compared to 100,000 from the West Riding; mass metropolitan support for Chartism became significant only during the 1840s. Support was limited in other areas. In Ireland, for example, there was suspicion on the part of the Catholic Church that Chartism would undermine society, and on the part of the Young Ireland movement because Chartism was English; this meant that its impact on Ireland was limited. Chartism gained little support in areas where Wesleyan Methodism was strong, as Methodist ministers spoke out strongly against the movement, and in Cornwall temperance and Methodist leaders combined to minimise Chartist influence. In other areas, by contrast, local nonconformists played a central role in the movement and some national leaders, like Henry Vincent, sought to give the movement a Christian rationale.

More generally, Chartism was weak in largely rural areas where deference and traditional forms of protest remained strong. In East Anglia, for instance, agricultural labourers in general were not convinced that winning the vote would remedy their economic position. In rural Wales, where the gap between rural and urban workers was to some extent bridged by their joint opposition to English dominance and their shared nonconformity, Chartism was paralleled by more traditional protest in the form of the Rebecca Riots against the toll charges of local turnpike trusts of 1839 and 1842.[3] Despite this regional and local diversity of Chartism, there was, however, a very real sense of national unity within the movement, especially in its peak years between 1839 and 1842, and also in 1848.

An occupational dimension

Occupational support for Chartism was also extensive: a wide range of urban and industrial workers was involved. Economic conditions were only partially responsible for this, although they were of major importance. Of the 23 local associations which responded to a questionnaire distributed by the 1839 Chartist Convention, only two stressed the lack of the vote as a general grievance; the majority complained of low wages, costly food, the scarcity of work and economic hardship. Considerable support came from domestic outworkers, while textile handloom-weavers, linen-spinners and wool-combers in Yorkshire, as well as silk-workers in Essex, were all chronically depressed in economic terms. It is significant that strong Chartist support was linked to the rising population, which placed additional pressure on low-skilled jobs within labour-intensive industries. Demands for a political answer to the economic grievances of working-class people were motivated not by the belief that the vote would improve their conditions, but that without it there could be no solution to their ills.

Factory workers played a far more active role in Chartism than in previous radical movements. Here too the initial motivation was economic, springing from the widespread unemployment of the late 1830s. Joseph Rayner Stephens was not alone in noting that Lancashire Chartism was a 'knife-and-fork question', but it was more than this. The early part of the century had seen long working hours offset by relatively high levels of wages; these had been weakened by technological change, especially by the introduction of the self-acting mule (a spinning machine) in the cotton textile industry. The economic slump of the late 1830s added to the factory workers' sense of frustration and despair.

The close association between trade unionism and Chartism in some areas has been regarded by some historians as showing unity of action among the working population.[4] However, trade unions now provided less support than they had earlier in the century and many factory workers turned – temporarily – to political agitation. Miners had also been previously insulated from other broadly popular movements, but during the late 1830s and early 1840s large numbers of them, especially in Wales and the West Midlands, became enmeshed in Chartism. In Staffordshire, however, miners' links with Chartism seem to have been more superficial: Chartists did play a prominent role in the organisation of the Plug Plot strikes of August 1842, but more importance was attached to the specific local grievances of the miners than to the Charter. By contrast, Chartists in south Wales were able to achieve a genuinely political agitation during 1838 and 1839 among both iron-workers and miners, which culminated in the abortive Newport Rising.

Factory workers and miners occupied an intermediate position between the rank-and-file outworkers and the artisans and small shopkeepers who formed most of the local Chartist leadership. In Suffolk and Essex, for example, tailors, shoemakers and building artisans looked to agricultural labourers for mass support; in Bath, artisans provided the leadership, and workers in the declining cloth trade the rank and file; in Aberdeen, there was a similar balance between handloom-weavers and a small and articulate artisan leadership. Craftsmen were prominent in the movement, partly because of their long tradition of political radicalism, but economic considerations gave the artisanal leadership an added edge. The growing market for relatively low-quality goods and the downward trend in prices compelled employers to cut their costs. This was responsible for the continuing expansion of the 'dishonourable' (or non-unionised) sector in traditional trades; the employment of unapprenticed and semi-skilled labour and a downward spiral into 'sweated' trades. Only a few skilled trades, like bookbinding and watch-making, were able to maintain their status and prosperity and therefore remained largely aloof from Chartism.

A gender dimension

Women were involved in Chartism to an unprecedented extent.[5] Yet, as Dorothy Thompson wrote, 'their presence has been virtually ignored by Chartism's historians'. She identifies three main reasons for this. Firstly, she argues that the movement's rank and file in most parts of the country has still not been closely studied, and where women played a significant role in Chartism, it was at a local, rather than national, level. Historians have tended to concentrate on Chartism as a national movement and, not surprisingly, the role of women within it has therefore been generally overlooked. Secondly, it is difficult to trace the identity of individual Chartists, and this is a far greater problem as regards women than men. The majority of the Chartist crowd of both sexes remained anonymous: we simply do not know who most of the Chartists were. Thirdly, there is the preoccupation of historians. The early historians, from R. C. Gammage to the Fabians, portrayed Chartism as a serious political movement. Tea parties, social occasions, Sunday schools, processions and other rituals which belonged to the older radical tradition, and within which women played a central role, did not fit into this rational mould and were thus either ignored or contrasted unfavourably with the modernity demonstrated by Chartism. Historians of women's movements have been equally dismissive of the role of Chartist women, largely because they were not seen as being specifically feminist.

Women played an important role in the early stages of the movement, in part motivated by their opposition to the perceived, if not actual, excesses of the new Poor Law. The 'Sisters in Bondage' – the female Chartists of Manchester – described theirs as a struggle for 'suitable houses, proper clothing and good food'. This concern with economic issues was also evident in references to 'pawn-brokers and furniture brokers' and to the spectre of unemployment: 'our husbands wandering the streets, willing to work but unable to procure it, thrown out in consequence of the improvements which have been made in machinery'. This strong female involvement – up to a third of those who signed the first petition in 1839 and also the petition on behalf of the transported John Frost in 1841 were women – was therefore not motivated primarily by the question of women's suffrage. Furthermore, although many Chartists advocated the vote for women, it was never part of the movement's programme. There is no suggestion that women considered themselves oppressed within their own families, neither is there any evidence of 'anti-male' agitation among the female Chartists. Women acted in support of their men and communities.

During the early years of the movement, there were almost 100 female radical associations, while a general commitment to both the extension of suffrage to women and the improvement of women's education was accepted by many radicals. By the mid-1840s, however, the radical press was mentioning women less, and the number of women in the crowd seems to have declined. The reasons for this withdrawal from politics on the part of women are unclear, although the decline of traditional forms of protest – the procession and the mass demonstration – and the development of the politics of the committee, Thompson argues, limited the role of women. This did not mean that women dropped out of the movement altogether, although the photograph of the Kennington Common meeting in April 1848 shows very few women. A further explanation may be that attitudes towards women tended to harden during the 1840s and there was a growing acceptance of the notion of 'separate [gender] spheres' by many working men, in theory if not always in practice. Such marginalising of women from the public domain and from skilled employment was an important element of the growing 'respectability' of working-class politics and life.

Social composition: some local examples

It is perfectly possible to make valid general statements about the social composition of Chartism during the 1830s and 1840s. However, what stands out is the diversity, richness and contradictory nature of the support for the movement, and this only becomes fully apparent on examining local examples. Three localities or regions, along with their respective traditions, will be used to illustrate this diversity: the rural Chartism of Essex and Suffolk; the metropolitan radicalism of London; and the provincial radicalism of Lancashire.

Rural Chartism: Essex and Suffolk

Local studies have focused on Chartism in the industrial and urban environment, and little has been written about its rural variant.[6] During this period, rural Britain retained its affection for the older forms of popular and social protest: the 1840s, for example, saw an increase in incidents of incendiarism and poaching across large parts of East Anglia.[7] There were also logistical problems: mass movements tend to be most effective where there is a concentration of population; this was not the case in rural Britain. The strength of the crowd lies, moreover, in part in its anonymity; in face-to-face rural society this did not exist. Pressure and intimidation from farmers and landlords also acted as an important restraint on radical activity. Furthermore, Chartism, with the possible exception of the Land Plan, simply did not appeal to many in rural Britain.

Essex and Suffolk were minor centres of Chartism between 1838 and 1848.[8] No local Chartist played any part in the movement's national leadership; on one occasion only did a local Chartist go as a delegate to a convention. Aware of the region's insignificance, one Ipswich member said, 'Suffolk is but a speck. The hardy sons of the North and Scotland are our hope.' Yet despite this, Chartist activity was reported in nearly 50 towns and villages. Large numbers of men and women attended Chartist meetings and hundreds acted as officials, committee members or speakers. Chartism in Suffolk and Essex may not have registered greatly within the national Chartist movement, but within its own localities it could not be ignored.

There was no large mass of industrial workers to provide the rank-and-file support; agricultural labourers were the dominant group among the working class and they faced a hostile agricultural establishment that wielded influence in the market towns as well as in the villages. Chartism never became a mass movement in these areas because it never received widespread or sustained support from agricultural labourers. Between 1838 and 1840 it gained a presence in several villages where less than 10,000 of the region's 80,000 farm labourers lived, but it retained this for at most a year and a half. Although it could count individual farm workers among its supporters, after 1840 they did not maintain branches in their own villages. No farm worker was ever recorded as having been a speaker or official. In rural Suffolk, leadership came from artisans – two tailors, a saddler, a shoemaker, a glover, a blacksmith, a weaver, a shopkeeper – as well as a country gentleman. Chartism was also unable to claim much industrial support: no workers, for example, took part in the Plug Plot general strike of August 1842. In fact, there were few industrial workers in Suffolk and Essex.

There was, however, support from the silk industry, and Chartism was an important force for 10 years at Braintree, Halstead, Coggeshall and Sudbury, whose silk-workers provided some of its leaders and most of the rank-and-file membership. Factory women, often the wives or daughters of weavers, played a limited role in organisational work, but between 1838 and 1839, and 1847 and 1848, they were well represented at public meetings. The silk industry's support may have reflected the economic trend, and the *Essex Standard* newspaper recognised a situation similar to that in the militant Chartist regions between 1847 and 1848, when Braintree's silk industry was affected by depression. Outside the silk industry, the largest factory was Ransomes at Ipswich which, until the mid-1840s, employed no more than 200 people. Neither this nor the other foundries at Leiston or Peasenhall was proved to have been the workplace of any local Chartist leader. Some individuals took out shares in the Land Company, but there was no comparable upsurge of support like that given at certain times by industrial workers in south Wales and the north. As for the ports, seaman and fishermen had never played a significant or regular role in public life, except for the few Brightlingsea fishermen who joined the Land Company in 1847.

There was no significant support for Chartism among the middle classes, except in 1838, when some liberals saw it as a stimulus for further reforms that had been promised in 1832 but had never been delivered. Certainly, some £10 householders (people living in towns who had been given the vote in 1832) belonged to the Ipswich Working Men's Association in early 1838, and there was a similar level of support in Braintree and Halstead. Middle-class support evaporated after 1839, however, leaving only those individuals involved who were local leaders: men like Flood, a Romford newsagent; Benjamin Parker, a Colchester fruiterer; Donald M'Pherson, an itinerant tea merchant; and George Bearman, who kept a beerhouse at Bocking. There is little evidence to suggest that such individuals were representative of their class, or that they had the support of more than a handful of their fellow tradesmen.

The absence of middle-class support for Chartism in Suffolk and Essex contrasts with the situation in other regions where, for example, Chartist success in municipal elections was partly due to the votes of middle-class rate-payers. The main reason for this lay in the dominance of the powerful agricultural establishment. Only four farmers are known to have been Chartist supporters. The majority of the region's middle classes supported those landowners and farmers who sternly opposed Chartism. This lack of middle-class support weakened Chartism in two respects. Firstly, the Chartists were severely restricted as regards the circles in which they could hope to extend their support, which resulted in Chartism remaining a minority movement, even in the towns. (It is, however, worth noting that Chartist strength in urban areas was stronger in east Suffolk and east Essex than in the western parts of those counties, where the towns were fewer and smaller.) Secondly, those individual middle-class people who were prepared to support the movement were significantly reduced after 1839. No middle-class regional leaders emerged who might have unified the separate branches, so creating an influential regional force.

Metropolitan Chartism: London

The metropolitan origins of Chartism and the events in the capital between 1838 and 1839 received considerable attention from the early historians of the movement. Yet, in 1960, Asa Briggs argued that there was still 'no account of Chartist activities in London'.[9] Later historians have begun to fill in the gaps. D. J. Rowe, for example, examined radicalism in London between 1829 and 1841,[10] focusing on the initial phase of Chartism in the capital, arguing correctly that the Spitalfields weavers and much of London's working class were apathetic, and assuming (wrongly) that this lack of interest continued into the 1840s. I. Prothero provided a useful corrective to Rowe's conclusions,[11] pointing to the diversity and continuity of London working-class radicalism but, by explicitly excluding 'mob activity and crowd psychology', almost totally neglecting London in 1848. David Large remedied this deficiency in an essay published in 1977.[12] It was not, however, until the publication of David Goodway's *London Chartism, 1838–1848* in 1982 and John Saville's *1848. The British state and the Chartist movement* five years later, that full-length studies devoted wholly or partly to Chartism in London appeared.

The People's Charter was published in May 1838, and during September and October 'monster' meetings were held throughout the country in order to adopt it and elect delegates for the planned Chartist Convention. The peak of London Chartism between 1838 and 1840 came at the meeting on 17 September 1838 which an estimated 15,000 attended; this number compares unfavourably with the 300,000 at Kersal Moor near Manchester. London Chartism moved away from the moderate LWMA towards the more radical London Democratic Association[13] (broadly an O'Connorite organisation) between September 1838 and the meeting of the convention the following February. In general, however, the reaction to Chartism in London during this period can only be called apathetic.[14] Goodway identifies three main reasons for this. Firstly, he suggests that there was a failure of leadership, especially among the LWMA, that did little to create rank-and-file support for the People's Charter. Secondly, he argues that London workers received higher wages than elsewhere and did not suffer from wage reductions or widespread unemployment between 1837 and 1839. Thirdly, unlike in northern England, where the anti-Poor Law movement had maintained radical activity and there was acute 'distress', mass radicalism had been dormant since the 'war of the unstamped' in 1836. Chartism therefore 'had to begin entirely from cold'.

Chartism began to take effective root in London in late 1840 and early 1841, and the metropolis remained a major Chartist stronghold throughout the 1840s.[15] The nature of the Chartist leadership changed with the emergence of a new group of militant activists which was O'Connorite in its approach. The metropolitan economy was hit by economic depression between 1841 and 1842, and this roused mass support for Chartism. The number of Chartist localities in London rose from 15 in April 1841, to 30 by the end of the year, and to 43 by the time of the Chartist Convention in April 1842. The *Northern Star* (the leading Chartist newspaper, controlled by O'Connor) reported in July 1842 that thousands were starving in Bermondsey and that half its shops were either up for let or entirely closed. James Epstein estimates that 8,000 Chartist membership cards had been taken out in London by the end of 1842; London was no longer apathetic.

After 1842, Chartist support in London – as in the rest of the country – declined as the economy revived. London, however, remained a major Chartist centre, and between 1843 and 1844 it became the headquarters for the *Northern Star*. Metropolitan Chartism was most dangerous in 1848 and posed a serious challenge to the state between March and June of that year. The familiar account of 1848 as being a year of 'fiasco' is therefore no longer acceptable or accurate.[16] If London's size was an important factor in Chartism, so were the stresses caused by its changing economy. Goodway argues that, in terms of absolute numbers, metropolitan Chartism was, when compared to other, less populous, strongholds, 'a failure', but that in terms of Chartist unity it was a 'remarkable success'.

The contemporary journalist Henry Mayhew drew a useful distinction between London's labourers and street folk, with their often ill-informed 'inclination' to Chartism, and the artisans who were 'almost to a man red-hot politicians'. There were some 50,000 labourers in London during the 1840s, who formed part of the crowd but little more. Like 'white-collar workers' – clerks, for example – they generally accepted their economic circumstances passively. The exception was the coal-whippers, who unloaded coal ships by jerking, or 'whipping', baskets of coal out of their holds and emptying them into barges alongside. By the summer of 1842 there were some 2,000 whippers in considerable distress; a general strike began on 24 August and by the end of October the men were still out on strike. The following year legislation was passed which regulated their working conditions; no standard rate of pay was conceded, but by 1851 average earnings of 16s (shillings) per week had regained their 1830 level. This reduced the coal-whippers' grievances significantly, and in 1848 many volunteered to act as special constables.

While Mayhew's understanding of the attitudes of London labourers is remarkably perceptive, subsequent historians have substantially modified his view of London artisans. There was a clear and divisive boundary between the 'honourable', or skilled, and the 'dishonourable', or semi-skilled, workers in the same trades. Skilled artisans sought to maintain their status and restrictive practices in the face of the employers' increasing use of workers who had not been through the process of apprenticeship. This skills' 'dilution' reflected the need of employers to expand their production and cut their costs. They achieved this in a variety of ways: some introduced machinery, though in general most industries remained largely unmechanised, a particular characteristic of London's industry; others employed cheaper, 'illegal' men. Work on the shop floor was replaced by low-skilled and low-paid home-working, promoting the 'sweated trades', which marginalised the economic role of many women. There were also some trades that were doing well while others were in decline.

The motivation for workers in London to become involved in Chartism was overwhelmingly economic. Almost every trade found itself under serious pressure from falling wages, the introduction of labour-saving machines, the emergence of 'sweating', and declining occupational status. What is clear is that there was considerable worker solidarity during the 1840s in their demands for political and social freedom. But there were limits. Co-operation was most powerful at the level of strikes and resistance to 'dilution'; it proved difficult to weld metropolitan craft-workers into a unified trades' council, however – this had to wait until 1860. The sectionalism of different trades and factionalism within trades therefore proved too great to overcome. Chartism, like trade unionism, was simply one means of achieving workers' aims and aspirations.

Provincial radicalism: Lancashire

Lancashire was at the heart of the 'Industrial Revolution'.[17] As towns and industries expanded, conflicts over wages or over demands for political reform intensified. Wage-earners, especially in the textile industries, began to combine in defence of their living standards almost a century before Chartism began. The reform crisis permanently raised the level of local political activity. Lancashire was given 12 additional parliamentary seats, its total rising to 26, but the working class formed only a small proportion of the urban electorate of £10 house-holders. The Reform Act of 1832 had raised the expectations of the organised working class in Lancashire and there were angry responses when the reformed parliament proved indifferent to petitions for further reform. Political activity remained intense in the years after 1832, after it became clear that the reformed parliament had little to offer working-class radicals.

The 1833 Factory Act also fell far short of the aspirations of the Lancashire committees on short-time working and demonstrated, for the first time, the shortcomings of the reformed parliament. There was additional widespread passive resistance to the 1834 Poor Law Amendment Act by employers and property owners, as well as by workers. Substantial hostility was voiced to directions from central government: the existing system, it was argued throughout Lancashire, was cheap and well-suited to the needs of the Lancashire economy. The cotton districts provided the focus for angry, and sometimes violent, working-class agitation against the new legislation. Riots against the new Poor Law guardians, for example, took place in Todmorden in 1838, and even middle-class opinion in Oldham and Rochdale was hostile to the new arrangements. In many trades, the 1830s and 1840s saw falling living standards, growing use of labour-saving machinery and ineffective trade-union action: wage reductions were imposed on the spinners between 1837 and 1842; hatters, tailors, fustian-cutters and calico-printers saw their unions broken in the 1830s. Powerloom-weavers, builders, metal-workers and miners were more successful, but only at a local level; attempts to build wider federations and national unions proved ineffective.

This catalogue of associated economic and political grievances was linked with the development of the new police forces and stronger forms of local government. Employers made up a significant proportion of Lancashire's MPs – by 1835 cotton employers had been returned for seven of the eight cotton constituencies – and they were also beginning to control the local magistracy. To many in the working class, this, combined with the indolence of the reformed parliament, increasingly looked like an establishment conspiracy against the non-voting working class, or of capital against labour. It was these conditions that created mass support for Chartism in Lancashire in 1838, and which sustained it into the 1840s and 1850s.

There were mass meetings at Kersal Moor and elsewhere in the later months of 1838, attracting thousands of supporters. However, the real importance of Lancashire to Chartism came in its second phase, when the movement regrouped after the setbacks of 1839 and 1840. By late 1841, one in six of the National Charter Association's (NCA's) branches were in Lancashire, thus putting the county on a par with the West Riding. The National Petition of 1842 was widely supported and Chartism reached its peak with the Plug Plot strikes of August 1842, after which its mass support quickly faded. There was a short-lived revival, however, with the return of trade depression and national agitation between 1847 and 1848. Indeed, Chartism did not disappear quickly, and local activists and groups existed into the 1850s and even the 1860s: in 1853, of the 58 provincial branches of the reconstructed NCA, 10 were in the cotton districts of Lancashire and the adjacent areas of Cheshire and Derbyshire; in 1854, 2,000 people attended a Chartist meeting on Blackstone Edge; and in 1858, 800 people crowded into the Chartist Institute at Staleybridge to hear Ernest Jones. Yet the Lancashire working class as an organised political force was virtually extinguished after 1848.

Chartism was strongest in the cotton-spinning factories around Manchester, especially if they were small and used outworkers like handloom-weavers. There was also substantial support in the small weaving villages of north-east Lancashire: in Sabden, for example, there were 44 subscribers to the *Northern Star* out of a total population of some 1,500. Manchester, as Asa Briggs has shown,[18] was the 'shock city' of the Industrial Revolution, but its factory population was dispersed, handloom-weavers did not make up a sizeable proportion of its working class and it was growing in importance as a commercial rather than manufacturing centre. This limited the impact of Chartism in Manchester.[19] Preston and Wigan, at the western edge of the cotton districts, saw little sustained or large-scale Chartist activity and Chartism made little headway outside the cotton districts. There is little evidence of support in Liverpool or in the mining and agricultural areas of south-west Lancashire.

Yet despite these qualifications, Chartism attracted a broad cross-section of working-class support. It is not surprising that there were strong links between Chartism and the vibrant local trade unions, especially between 1838 and 1839, and in 1842.[20] Factory workers were active, especially in the local Chartist leadership, and they were supported by handloom-weavers and artisans. Unlike in London, Lancashire Chartism also appealed to shopkeepers, small tradesmen and even some textile employers.

Chartism brought together overlapping and contradictory political ideologies in Lancashire. The traditionalists (largely artisans) attacked the 'Old Corruption' in church and state; the broadly middle-class analysis of political economy denounced protective policies, especially the Corn Laws; while the working class assailed its exploitation and domination by employers and the government particularly regarding the Poor Law, the legal status of trade unions and the operation of the labour market. These working-class concerns split the radical constituency, however. Middle-class reformers were disturbed by the extreme rhetoric and the attempted rising of 1839; those who believed in freeing trade were opposed to trade unions and saw the repeal of the Corn Laws as a more achievable objective than the Charter. Indeed, the Anti-Corn Law League was very successful in winning over moderate and middle-class Chartists. Many radical free-traders were also nonconformists whose priorities were pointed more towards temperance, self-improvement and the battle against tithes and church rates than towards the resolution of expressly working-class problems. A committed core of working-class Chartists remained, but after 1842 they lost most of their middle-class support and most of their potential for mass mobilisation.

The revival of the economy after 1842 played a major role in reducing the political temperature in Lancashire. The repeal of the Corn Laws in 1846 and the 1847 Factory Act showed that central government was now able to respond positively to pressure from the provinces, which directly challenged the Chartist ideology that the state was both hopelessly corrupt and incapable of making concessions to the working class. Three other tentative reasons for the decline of Chartism in Lancashire can be advanced. Firstly, at least in Oldham in 1847, the mainstream Whig and Tory parties were bidding for both middle- and working-class radical support by playing on religious and cultural divisions. Secondly, the historian John Foster argues that working-class anger was diverted from the employers: Irish immigrants, whose numbers ballooned during the 1840s, became the focus of working-class antagonism, both on account of their Catholicism and because they were a pool of cheap labour. Thirdly, the 1840s saw a revival of employer paternalism that aimed to bridge the gap between labour and capital.

There are, however, problems with each of these suggestions. The anti-Catholicism directed against Irish immigrants, for example, occurred during the 1850s and 1860s rather than during the 1840s, while it is difficult to assess the impact of employer paternalism on working-class attitudes. Certainly, class relations stabilised during the 1850s, and there was a growing separation between the political action and industrial conflict that had, for example, characterised the strikes of 1842. There were also improved opportunities for upward social mobility within sections of the working class, that were encouraged by institutions like friendly societies and the co-operative movement, as well as through the development of self-help as an alternative ideology.

Conclusions

Historians face considerable difficulty in analysing the social make-up of Chartism. The size of the movement, its longevity and the limited availability of evidence regarding its rank-and-file members, supporters and sympathisers add to this problem. It is sometimes difficult to fathom why support for Chartism in one area was particularly strong while in others it was not. Local leadership, the attitude of local employers and the lower-middle classes, local economic conditions and local sources of working-class grievances, for example, all played an important part in determining and maintaining popular support for Chartism. Local and regional studies make very clear that, while it may be valid to call Chartists collectively 'the union of the productive classes', it is essential to recognise the diversity of social responses and motivations within the movement. The Chartist movement may be said to have been based on a kernel of demands that were, by definition, national; this undoubtedly united Chartists in a national community of purpose but, at its heart, the Chartist experience was essentially a local, and largely anonymous, one.

Document case study
The metropolitan dilemma

2.1 Chartist attitudes

. . . unless the metropolis be set working, all agitation elsewhere is useless. It is here that the seat of Government is. A demonstration in the streets of London comes before the very eyes of those who make the law. An atmosphere of agitation here does not dissipate without first involving the two houses of legislation in its influence.

Source: *The Chartist*, 30 June 1839

2.2 Place to Cobden

London differs very widely from Manchester, and, indeed, from every other place on the face of the earth. It has no local or particular interest as a town, not even as to politics. Its several boroughs in this respect are like so many very populous places at a distance from one another, and the inhabitants of any one of them know nothing, or next to nothing, of the proceedings in any other, and not much indeed of those of their own . . . isolated as men are here, living as they do at considerable distances, many seven miles apart, and but seldom meeting together, except in small groups, to talk either absolute nonsense on miserable party politics or to transact business exclusive to everything else.

Source: Francis Place to Richard Cobden, 4 March 1840, on the expectations for the Anti-Corn Law League in London; printed in full in Graham Wallas, *The life of Francis Place*, revised edn, London, 1918, pp. 393–94

2.3 *Northern Star*

London is always the last to stir, or when it takes the initiative, such is its overwhelming bulk, and the consequent segregation of its parts, that no powerful and well compacted concentration of popular energy is produced . . . When you do get a large meeting it is not London, but the friendly parties who reside in different parts of it that are brought together by a common feeling. The outer public is scarcely stirred. How different all this is in a provincial town! [Agitation] . . . must be rolled up to London from the country.

Source: *Northern Star*, 21 December 1850, cited in D. Read, *The English provinces*, London, 1964, pp. 116–17

2.4 The first Chartist Convention, 1839

. . . there was not sufficient consideration for the position of London, which possessed many conflicting interests, where the people were strangers to each other, engaged day and night in their various trades; whereas the people of manufacturing cities knew each other individually. There are other causes . . . the enormous extent of the city prevents the people assembling and acting . . . The working men could not be concentrated so easily as the people of the country.

Source: Robert Hartwell addressing the first Chartist Convention, printed in *Operative*, 31 March 1839, cited in D. Goodway, *London Chartism, 1838–1848*, Cambridge, 1982, p. 224

2.5 A commentary from the 1850s

Those who shudder at the idea of an outbreak in the metropolis containing two millions and a half of people and at least fifty thousand of the 'dangerous classes' forget that the capital is so wide that its different sections are totally unknown to each other. A mob in London is wholly without cohesion, and the individuals composing it have but few feelings, thoughts or pursuits in common.

Source: cited in D. Goodway, *London Chartism, 1838–1848*, Cambridge, 1982, p. 223

Document case-study questions

1 In what respects does 2.1 justify the importance of London in political agitation during the late 1830s? Why did political leadership not emerge in London in the years between 1838 and 1840?

2 2.3 refers to Londoners being brought together by 'common feeling'. Why was common feeling not translated into effective political action?

3 How far does 2.5 contradict 2.3, and why?

4 2.2, 2.3 and 2.4 each draw unfavourable comparisons between radicalism in London and in the provinces. How do they justify this position?

5 How far do these five sources explain why the development of Chartism in London proved difficult?

6 'The diverse experiences of the working population in London during the 1830s and 1840s largely explain why Chartism made little impact on it in the early stages of the movement.' Discuss.

Notes and references

1 *Christian Socialist*, vol. 2, no. 59, 13 (December 1851), extracts printed in Dorothy Thompson, *The early Chartists*, London, 1971, pp. 82–86.

2 The most extensive general discussion of the question 'Who were the Chartists?' is to be found in Dorothy Thompson, *The Chartists: popular politics in the Industrial Revolution*, Aldershot, 1984, pp. 91–236.

3 The best examination of the Rebecca Riots is David J. V. Jones, *Rebecca's children: a study of rural society, crime and protest*, Oxford, 1989.

4 R. Sykes, 'Early Chartism and trade unionism', in James Epstein and Dorothy Thompson (eds.), *The Chartist experience: studies in working-class radicalism and culture, 1830–1860*, London, 1982; John Rule, *The labouring classes in early industrial England, 1750–1850*, London, 1986, pp. 310–42 on craft unionism, miners and Chartism provides a useful starting point on this contentious issue.

5 Thompson, *The Chartists*, pp. 120–51 is invaluable. David Jones, 'Women and Chartism', *History*, vol. 68 (1983), is less critical. Jutta Schwarzkopf, *Women in the Chartist movement*, London, 1991, is a more detailed, though not entirely satisfactory, study.

6 Hugh Fearn and R. B. Pugh contributed essays on Chartism in Suffolk, Somerset and Wiltshire to Asa Briggs (ed.), *Chartist studies*, London, 1959; and, more recently, see Roger Wells, 'Southern Chartism', *Rural History*, vol. 2 (1991), reprinted in J. Rule and R. Wells, *Crime, protest and popular politics in southern England, 1740–1850*, London, 1997.

7 On rural radicalism, see A. J. Peacock, 'Village radicalism in East Anglia, 1800–50', in J. P. D. Dunbabin, *Rural discontent in nineteenth-century Britain*, London, 1974.

8 For the analysis on Essex and Suffolk, I have relied heavily on A. E. J. Brown, *Chartism in Essex and Suffolk*, Chelmsford, 1982.

9 Asa Briggs, 'Open questions of labour history', *Bulletin of the Society for the Study of Labour History*, no. 1 (autumn 1960), p. 2, quoted in David Goodway, *London Chartism, 1838–1848*, Cambridge, 1982, p. xiii.

10 D. J. Rowe, 'Radicalism in London, 1829–1841: with special reference to its middle- and working-class components', unpublished MA thesis, University of Southampton, 1965; 'The London Working Men's Association and the People's Charter', *Past and Present*, vol. 36 (1967); and 'The London Working Men's Association and the People's Charter – rejoinder', *Past and Present*, vol. 38 (1967).

11 I. Prothero, 'London working-class movements, 1825–1848', unpublished PhD thesis, University of Cambridge, 1967; 'The London Working Men's Association and the "People's Charter"', *Past and Present*, vol. 38 (1967); and 'Chartism in London', *Past and Present*, vol. 44 (1969).

12 David Large, 'London in the year of revolution, 1848', in John Stevenson (ed.), *London in the age of reform*, Oxford, 1977, pp. 177–212.

13 On this, see Jennifer Bennett, 'The London Democratic Association, 1837–41: a study in London radicalism', in Epstein and Thompson (eds.), *The Chartist experience*, pp. 87–119.

14 Goodway, *London Chartism*, pp. 24–37.

15 Goodway, *London Chartism*, pp. 37–53.

16 Goodway, *London Chartism*, pp. 68–87, 111–23, 129–41.

17 John K. Walton, *Lancashire: a social history, 1558–1939*, Manchester, 1987, is a good starting point.

18 In his *Victorian cities*, London, 1963, p. 56, Briggs wrote: 'If Chicago was the "shock city" of the 1890s, one of the British nineteenth-century cities – Manchester – was the shock city of the 1840s, attracting visitors from all countries, forcing to the surface what seemed to be intractable problems of society and government, and generating as great a variety of opinions as Chicago did later or Los Angeles did in the 1930s and 1940s. Every age has its shock city.'

19 Paul A. Pickering, *Chartism and the Chartists in Manchester and Salford*, London, 1995, is essential.

20 Robert Sykes, 'Early Chartism and trade unionism in south-east Lancashire', in Epstein and Thompson (eds.), *The Chartist experience*, is invaluable on this.

The Chartist leadership

R. C. Gammage's *The history of the Chartist movement* established the orthodoxy on Chartist leadership that was to last well into the twentieth century. His judgements on George Julian Harney, Ernest Jones and especially Feargus O'Connor were uniformly hostile and unflattering, while in his hands William Lovett, Henry Vincent and Bronterre O'Brien were portrayed as the prudent, astute and forward-thinking leaders of the movement: 'physical force' versus 'moral force'. Gammage was, however, far from being an impartial observer: he was 35 when he wrote his history and had himself been active in the latter stages of the movement, having been greatly involved in its quarrels and disputes and seeing O'Connor as its main cause of failure. The emergence of the study of labour history in the early years of the twentieth century reinforced this view of the Chartist leadership. Mark Hovell and other, essentially Fabian, writers viewed O'Connor in a critical light but raised the profile of the reformist ideology of William Lovett. Marxists, too, were critical of O'Connor; he had to wait until 1982 before James Epstein produced a revisionist interpretation of his role, at least up to 1842, in *The lion of freedom*.[1]

The publication in 1941 of G. D. H. Cole's *Chartist portraits* marked an important shift in approach. His chosen 12 individuals illustrate the problems of examining leadership within Chartism. He did not choose Henry Vincent, the orator who stirred south Wales and the west in 1839, for example, because of the overlap with John Frost of the Newport Rising. Others, like the radical bookseller James Watson, were not included because, as in the case of Watson, their lives did not illustrate 'any clearly defined phase or aspect of the Chartist movement'. Cole left out the leaders of Scottish Chartism because he 'did not know enough about any of them', and the Irishmen of 1848 because it 'would have taken me too far afield'. There was also the problem of insufficient available information: Simeon Pollard of Yorkshire, Cole suggested, fell into this category. He argued that there was 'room for a dozen local studies in Chartism, and for a dozen biographies . . . of outstanding Chartist leaders'.[2] Five decades later, there are ample biographies but still no synoptic analysis of the Chartist leadership. Before examining the role of three particular 'leaders', I want to consider in general terms what 'Chartist leadership' actually means.

Political leadership: a tentative typology

In 1841, Thomas Carlyle published his work *On heroes, hero-worship and the heroic in history*. For Carlyle, heroes were set apart by their strength of character, which let them shape events rather than simply react to them. This gave them a moral superiority that was both capable of uniting people and allowed them to act as role models in a divisive society. William Lovett, in his autobiography published in 1876, echoed Carlyle's views when he wrote:

> They [the working classes] were always looking up *to leadership* of one description of another; were being swayed to and fro in opinion and action by the *idol* of their choice, and were rent and divided when some popular breath had blown that *idol* from its pedestal. In fact the masses, in their political organisations, were taught to look up to *'great men'* (or to men *professing greatness*) rather than to great principles.[3]

James Vernon argues that 'In a world devoid of the "stars" of mass entertainment and organised sport, [political leaders] occupied a (possibly the) central place in popular culture, at once revered and reviled, loved and loathed.'[4]

Political leaders quickly learned that they needed to present themselves in different ways to different people; they needed a sense of audience. The working class in the nineteenth century venerated its leaders as heroes and as potent icons. Birthdays, prison releases or simply a local visit were all sufficient reason for a celebration to honour the hero and to shower him with gifts. A sense of devotion and awe can also be seen in contemporary ballads and songs. Oratory, too, encouraged the glorification of leaders: as James Vernon puts it, 'Those blessed with the gift of the gab appeared natural leaders, their commanding presence on a platform, their ability to keep audiences enthralled, conveyed the impression of men in control of their own destinies, shaping, not reacting to the course of events.'[5] The 'marketing' of leaders was also important, and this required access to, and ideally control of, their own newspapers or journals. James Bronterre O'Brien, Feargus O'Connor and Ernest Jones all used their respective papers to get their particular messages across, as well as to report their sufferings and successes to a national audience that would absorb them. This allowed a strong sense of personal familiarity to develop between the Chartist leaders and the masses. The political memorabilia of the day – portraits, statuettes and figurines – illustrates the popularity of leaders, as well as their iconic importance; such objects were the nineteenth-century equivalent of today's posters, and were often highly personal.

Yet leadership is an elusive and controversial concept.[6] Political leadership is something which many today view with cynicism. Certainly, the historiography of Chartism is saturated with historians who took a hostile view of the nature of the Chartist leadership. O'Connor, for example, was branded at worst a demagogue, at best a democrat; Lovett, a conciliator acting pragmatically to achieve his objectives.

How can the historian best characterise the Chartist 'leader'? The archetypal leader was a 'politician' who sought the will and the welfare of 'the people'. He saw himself as the spokesman for, and leader of, a social group from which he drew his energy and moral authority. He fed on group approval. Drama was essential: roles had to be played out. The task of the Chartist leader was therefore easiest when agreement was clear, difficult when agreement was unclear, and most difficult when unanimity appeared compromised. In relation to this, 'image' was of primary importance. Different images of the leader – the father, the martyr, the fighter, the hero – were presented as and when necessary. Above all, the Chartist leader needed to ingratiate himself with his supporting constituency. He was, in part, a charismatic figure; however, his popularity was bound up in perceptions of the accuracy of his interpretation of the group's values and aspirations. But the chemistry of group support was notoriously fickle and the actions of leaders could easily be misread. It followed that the Chartist leader was necessarily committed to a heavy schedule of personal contact with his supporters. He could not afford to neglect this, nor could he afford to be aloof: he had to be busily engaged in a continuous series of making and maintaining personal contacts; he had to sustain consensus. This could prove difficult, however, for the line between seeking and manipulating consensus was often difficult to draw. Group membership fluctuated and group values provided only a short-lasting unity: better economic conditions, alternative social groupings, fragmented ideology – all contributed to the decline of support for the leader.

Classifying the leadership patterns within the Chartist movement is essential if the archetypal framework is to have real meaning. It is possible to view Chartist leaders in three major ways:

1 within a geographical dimension;
2 according to their leadership characteristics;
3 with regard to the fluidity of leadership.

The geographical dimension

Firstly, there was an important geographical dimension: leaders tended to be national, regional or local in their appeal to the working class. O'Connor is the classic example of a national figure pulling together the diverse elements of the movement. Regional leaders were significant within the particular areas of the country where their own social and economic structures and political traditions prevailed. Joseph Rayner Stephens was primarily concerned with the north of England, for example; William Lovett is perhaps best understood in relation to London; while Henry Vincent was characterised as the 'Demosthenes [the fourth-century BC Athenian orator and statesman] of the West' in 1839. Local leaders pose the greatest problem for historians, however. Some, like Thomas Cooper of Leicester, were their own publicists or, like John Frost, the former mayor of Newport, became national celebrities, but despite this, most are little known. Yet, in their day, individuals like Joshua Hobson of Leeds played a major part in the development of the movement. Hobson had links with Richard Oastler, Robert Owen and O'Connor. His newspaper, *Voice of the West Riding*, helps to explain much of the content of the *Northern Star*; indeed, he was the main publisher of the *Northern Star* from its beginnings in 1837 until it was moved to London in 1844.

Leadership characteristics

Secondly, we may consider Chartist leaders in relation to particular leadership characteristics. It is important to recognise from the outset that these 'types' are not all-inclusive: an individual may straddle two or more of the different categories. It is possible to identify four main leadership characteristics within Chartism, as follows.

1 *Ideologues*. These individuals provided the theoretical foundation on which Chartism was built. Three are particularly important: James Bronterre O'Brien, George Julian Harney and Ernest Jones. Bronterre O'Brien and Harney both based their theorisation on the achievements of the French Revolution. O'Brien supported the nationalisation of land and, by extending the principle to all monopolies of capital as well, became a pioneer of collectivism. Harney became a leading exponent of internationalism on a proletarian basis. Ernest Jones took a socialist route, at least during the 1850s, when he became a leading light of British Marxism.

2 *Activists*. These were individuals, such as William Cuffay in London, Richard Pilling in Manchester and William Benbow, who were good at the type of organisation required for handling a local or regional group. Their talent lay in organising things in a practical, rather than theoretical, way. They were able to take into account the realities of human nature and of fluctuating enthusiasm. They were determined to keep Chartism alive and, in addition, were sensitive to the way in which things were going.

3 *Communicators*. These were individuals who were good at communicating with others, either face to face or through some other medium. Henry Hetherington, James Watson and George Jacob Holyoake fall into this broad category.

4 *Leaders*. These individuals liked taking responsibility and making decisions. They were those who found leadership a natural role. In many respects, leaders are good at making things happen, providing the direction and determination to get things done as well as the skill to overcome obstacles. Leadership is a personality characteristic more than an intellectual one. The newspaper *Reynolds Miscellany* proclaimed as late as 1848: 'Feargus [O'Connor] is irresistible. He has great declaratory powers but he is wholly destitute of original ability. He declaims admirably; but he would not do for debate. He has vast energy . . . and energy always tells well in a speaker, especially a popular speaker.'

The fluidity of leadership

Finally, leadership was fluid within the Chartist movement: it changed over time. Mapping the Chartist leaders of 1839, 1842 and 1848 reveals significant changes in personnel. Although some leaders, like O'Connor, were involved in all three phases, others, like Attwood, passed from the scene, and most were involved in only one or two phases of the movement. This lack of political continuity, rather than the quality of management itself, may help to explain some of the inadequacies of its leadership across the course of the movement.

Three Chartist leaders

Which leaders is it best to include? I have chosen William Lovett and Thomas Cooper because they wrote autobiographies in which they sought to establish their radical credentials, as well as justifying their own attitudes to the Chartist movement. Feargus O'Connor is also discussed, and is further explored by means of the document case study and questions at the end of the chapter.

William Lovett

William Lovett (1800–77) is one of the most highly regarded working-class leaders of the nineteenth century. His place in the upper echelons of working-class radicals has been ensured by the praise of successive historians of the labour political movement.[7] R. H. Tawney viewed him as a 'social democrat' and as the first and greatest of the working-class educationalists; G. D. H. Cole saw him as an idealist. Among the older school of historians, only Marxists like Theodore Rothstein have differed from this verdict, on the grounds of Lovett's ineffectiveness and his lack of revolutionary perspective, rather than because of his basic goals.[8] Today, historians are more aware of the intricacies of working-class radicalism than they were when such commentators as Hovell, Cole and Tawney were writing. The labels traditionally commonly attached to Lovett and O'Connor, as exemplars of moral and physical force respectively, have crumbled under the onslaught of revisionist interpretations of Chartism. As Joel Wiener, Lovett's most recent biographer, concludes:

> he possessed an unusual measure of integrity and believed throughout his life in justice for the working classes. He fought hard to improve their lot . . . He possessed a zeal and enthusiasm that held up well in the face of many discouraging setbacks. He was a pioneer and a plodder where other reformers lacked the stamina to continue to pursue a better life. If Lovett was neither as great a man as some of his supporters contend nor as insignificant as several recent detractors maintain, he was nonetheless an unusual and outstanding reformer: one who made permanent contributions to working-class politics and education.[9]

Lovett's autobiography, *The life and struggles of William Lovett in pursuit of bread, knowledge and freedom,* was first published in 1876, barely a year before his death. It is a classic account of working-class life. This autobiography promoted or – as Wiener suggests, 'confused' – Lovett's own cause. His narrative is persuasive, but Lovett omitted or reinterpreted material that was unfavourable to him. His discussion of the first Chartist Convention, for example, is unexpectedly slight; the work is on occasions inconsistent and certainly self-congratulatory. Yet it is one of the major sources for the study of Chartism. Wiener argues – I think correctly – that it 'overshadows all other sources', although it is less illuminating on the earlier and later phases of his life.[10] The 'confusion' that Wiener refers to arises less from what Lovett wrote about himself – it is not surprising that an autobiography should be concerned with self-justification, or that something written decades after the events that it describes should be partial – but from the ways in which historians have interpreted it. Lovett's actions have been regarded as being moderate by most labour historians, especially those writing before the 1970s.

But there is a certain pettiness in the autobiography, as well as vindictiveness, especially in his denunciation of O'Connor. The animosity between the two men had both temperamental and political causes, and had its roots in London's radical politics of the early 1830s: it was before, not after, the People's Charter was drafted, for example, that O'Connor condemned Lovett's LWMA and Lovett attacked O'Connor for 'self-idolatry'. There is also rhetorical violence in Lovett's language, at least until the early 1840s: 'Shall it be said, fellow-countrymen, that four million of men, capable of bearing arms, and defending their country against every foreign assailant, allowed a few domestic oppressors to enslave and degrade them?'[11]

His autobiography clearly reveals Lovett's limitations as a radical leader. He was, at heart, a London radical who believed that Chartism was a means of continuing earlier demands for parliamentary reform as a step towards the form of political democracy that had begun in the mid-eighteenth century. Furthermore, the LWMA was an extremely small group: Hovell suggested that the total number of members admitted between June 1836 and 1839 was 279. Unlike O'Connor, Lovett did not understand the north; much as he may have despised the new industrialism, it largely passed him by. Lovett's schoolmasterly approach made little impact on many Chartist supporters in the north, for it had little appeal to the casualties of capitalism. The magic of Chartism for these people arose from its revolt against capitalism. O'Connor's oratory, and his understanding of the misery and despair of the northern industrial worker, thus allowed him to snatch the leadership of the Chartist movement out of the hands of Lovett and London in 1839. O'Connor was helped in this because Lovett was in prison for sedition from August 1839 to July 1840. While imprisoned, Lovett wrote, with John Collins, *Chartism: a new organisation of the people*. Its stress on the need for education and organisation within the movement was nothing new: these had long been basic tenets of radicalism. As soon as the book was published and Lovett had made his first efforts to implement its provisions, however, it was vehemently attacked in the *Northern Star*. Lovett commented: '*Education* was ridiculed, Knowledge was sneered at, *Facts* were perverted, *Truth* suppressed, and the lowest passions and prejudices of the multitude was appealed to, to obtain a clamorous verdict against us.'[12]

Lovett was always at his rhetorical best when personally attacked. He returned to London and founded a new organisation – the National Association of the United Kingdom for Promoting the Social and Political Improvement of the People – to continue the agitation for the People's Charter. On its behalf, he also attended the abortive Complete Suffrage conference that was summoned by Joseph Sturge in 1842 in the hope of uniting reformers of both the working and middle classes. Lovett's 'new move' was condemned by O'Connor and by the main organ of the Chartist movement, the National Charter Association (NCA). Lovett had moved irremediably to the fringes of the Chartist movement. He helped to found the Democratic Friends of All Nations later in the 1840s and the People's League, an abortive attempt to unite working- and middle-class radicals, in 1848. Lovett's policy was to work for gradual reform through the pressure of public opinion; he was prepared to consider 'ulterior measures' as a last resort. Yet he believed that one principal cause of the defeat of Chartism was that the promoters of confrontation drove many supporters away from the movement, and that O'Connor's rhetoric was 'morally in collision' with authority.

So where did Lovett stand in relation to the ideology of Chartism? His position is made very clear in the manifestos that he wrote, and later printed, in his autobiography. R. H. Tawney identified four propositions that were at the heart of Lovett's thinking, as follows:

1 Lovett recognised that social evils were the consequence of social institutions and therefore believed that the former could be removed by altering the latter.
2 The cause of social evils was government by a political oligarchy, which had an interest in maintaining them. The destruction of this oligarchy was to be achieved by parliamentary reform in which manhood suffrage was a natural right. The existing system, Lovett believed, was a distortion of the spirit of the constitution.
3 A national system of education was a primary condition of any genuine democracy. From the mid-1840s, Lovett's educational work increasingly absorbed his attention and he gradually separated from his old allies.
4 Lovett argued that the cause of democracy was international. He attacked the existing international system that allowed European governments to take common action to suppress all reform movements. He argued that the tyranny from which the working classes suffered in England was the same as that which afflicted Ireland. In 1844 Lovett therefore helped to found the Democratic Friends of All Nations, which was composed of English radicals and exiles from France, Germany and Poland. This internationalism was a particular characteristic of Chartism, and the LWMA was the first English organisation to produce manifestos for foreign use.

Until the mid-1840s, Lovett's radical vision continued to be that of a skilled artisan. He expressed the claims of the working classes within the 'us' versus 'them' framework of the old radical tradition. He felt anger at the wrongs suffered by the poor. Working-class self-improvement, self-help and class-consciousness were, in Lovett's view, the keys to political reform. By the 1850s, Lovett was taking an increasingly 'respectable' and 'liberal' stance. These changes in attitude can be seen particularly in his views on women's suffrage. During the 1830s, Lovett was a radical promoter of women's rights: in the first draft of the People's Charter, for example, he argued that women should be entitled to the vote. Indeed, he was committed to universal political rights when most radicals were not. Yet by the late 1840s Lovett had become more conventional in his attitudes: he believed in educating women so that they would be capable of training their sons to be model reformers. By the 1850s he was entirely conventional in his thinking.

Thomas Cooper

Thomas Cooper was 67 when his autobiography was published in 1872; by then, he had been an itinerant Baptist preacher for almost 14 years. *The Life of Thomas Cooper* has been called 'a perceptive account of a vigorous personality'.[13] Although Cooper tried to be objective about his past, there is no doubt that he was not always successful in this: he was proud of the part that he had played in national politics during the 1840s, and of his reputation as a renowned Chartist poet, but 'Thomas Cooper, the preacher' found it difficult to acknowledge the political record of militancy of 'Thomas Cooper, the Chartist'. G. D. H. Cole summed up the problem: 'no one, reading it and knowing nothing else about him, would get a correct picture of him as he had been in his Chartist prime', for he 'could not help making himself out as having been, politically, a good deal more dove-like than he had been in fact'.[14]

Thomas Cooper was born in Leicester in 1805.[15] His formative years are important for three reasons.

1 He had learned to read by the age of three and his passion for learning was perhaps the most sustained enthusiasm of his life. Between 1828 and 1829, and 1833 and 1838, he was a schoolmaster, first in Gainsborough and then in Lincoln.
2 He was apprenticed to a cobbler and from 1820 to 1827 worked regularly as a shoemaker.
3 He was converted to Baptist Christianity, initially during the Primitive Methodist revival in 1818 and later by the Wesleyan Methodists in 1829. For five years he was a local preacher and, although he quarrelled with the Wesleyans and moved towards a form of secularism in the 1840s, he retained the revivalist fervour of his youth, which was put to good use as a Chartist.

Cooper turned to part-time journalism on the *Lincoln, Rutland and Stamford Mercury* newspaper, and in 1838 closed his school and moved briefly to Stamford and then to London. Eventually, in 1840, he moved to Leicester to take up a post at the local Whig-liberal *Leicestershire Mercury*.

The first phase of Chartism had passed Cooper by. He was already radically minded by 1840, but it was his experience of poverty in London, and his initial contact with the stocking-frame workers of Leicester, that converted him to Chartism. Local Chartists proposed that he take over the editorship of the *Midland Counties Illuminator* newspaper, and he also began lecturing on behalf of the movement on Sunday evenings. These years of the early 1840s illustrate Cooper's temperament: his ability to organise (in stark contrast to Lovett); his difficulty in working with others; his unlimited enthusiasm for the movement; and his inclination to hero-worshipping. The rift between O'Connor and Lovett was replicated in Leicester, and Cooper emerged as the leading supporter of O'Connor: R. C. Gammage described him as 'O'Connor mad'.

Appointed one of Leicester's delegates to the Manchester conference of the NCA in August 1842, Cooper left Leicester on 9 August and, on his way to Manchester, spoke at Birmingham, Wednesbury, Bilton and Stafford. He then went on to the Staffordshire Potteries, where he addressed a series of meetings that culminated in a great open-air rally at Hanley. Like Joseph Rayner Stephens, Cooper used strong language: the familiar tool of revivalist preaching. The evening after he left Hanley there was widespread rioting and burning of houses and Cooper was arrested on the charge of incitement to arson and held in Stafford jail from late August to October. Cooper was acquitted of the charge, but his speeches may well have had the effect of rousing the people of the Potteries to riot. He was re-arrested on a charge of sedition immediately after his acquittal, but was granted bail, which enabled him to take part in the Complete Suffrage conference in Birmingham in December 1842.

Initially, Cooper had taken a positive view of the Complete Suffrage movement, and had argued for unity between the middle and working classes. He then veered, under O'Connor's influence, to opposing the middle-class radicals. Yet the collapse of the strike movement after August 1842 led to a further redefinition of his position: clearly, working-class action alone was not going to get the Charter accepted; working with the middle classes seemed a better option. At the December conference, Cooper seconded an attempt to have both the Sturgeite bill of rights – incorporating the 'six points' – and the People's Charter accepted as a basis for a national petition to parliament. This compromise was not accepted, however, and the conference broke up in disarray. Cooper then returned to Leicester to prepare for his trial for sedition. Found guilty in March 1843, he was finally sentenced to two years' imprisonment in May. Cooper emerged from prison in early 1845 a good deal more moderate in his politics. His autobiography mentions his political activities after his release only briefly.

Cooper remained a very political person within the framework of 'moral-force' Chartism. He had, however, not yet broken away from the main Chartist body, and was elected as one of the London delegates to the Chartist Convention in 1846, where the violence of his opposition to O'Connor exploded and led to his expulsion. This ended Cooper's association with the official Chartist movement, and he held aloof from the Chartist revival in 1848, concentrating instead on education and journalism and eventually again on the religion of his youth.

Following Cooper's death in 1892, George Julian Harney suggested in an obituary in the *Newcastle Weekly Chronicle* that Cooper, like Lovett, was a frustrated man. The reasons for this frustration, however, differed. Lovett possessed a considerable degree of certainty: even when he turned away from Chartism, he still maintained his belief in the principles of the Charter; the issue was never whether or not the Charter was right, but how best to implement it. Cooper lacked this spiritual certainty.

Feargus O'Connor

Feargus O'Connor was born in 1796 in Connorville, County Cork, in Ireland, and died in 1855 in London. After practising law, he entered politics in 1832, when he was elected a member of parliament for County Cork. Unseated in 1835, he then turned to radical political agitation in England, although he continued to press for the resolution of Irish grievances and to seek, though with little success, Irish support. As a result of his oratory and energy, O'Connor became the best-known Chartist leader and the movement's most popular and effective speaker. His journal, the *Northern Star*, founded in 1837, gained a wide circulation. O'Connor's methods and views alienated other Chartist leaders, particularly William Lovett, but in 1841 – after spending a year in prison for seditious libel – he became the undisputed leader of the movement. His failure to lead the movement to victory in 1842 and 1848, his vacillating attitudes towards the middle class and eventually towards the People's Charter, his obsession with the Land Plan, and the emergence of younger leaders with new ideas, resulted in the start of his loss of power, although he was elected as a member of parliament for Nottingham in 1847. The failure of the People's Charter in 1848 marked the beginning of the end for O'Connor, however, who was becoming increasingly unstable. Declared insane in 1852, he died three years later.

Commentators' attitudes to O'Connor and the contribution he made to the Chartist movement tended, until recently, to be extremely negative. Gammage was highly critical of him, and Lovett regarded O'Connor as the major cause of the failure of the movement. Such contemporary attitudes were taken up by the early historians of the movement, and remained the orthodox position until the 1970s. More recent historians, especially James Epstein,[16] have taken a more dispassionate view of O'Connor's role, however.

Document case study
Feargus O'Connor

3.1 Lovett on O'Connor

I regard Fergus [*sic*] O'Connor as the chief marplot [spoiler] of our movement . . . a man, who, by his personal conduct joined to his malignant influence in the *Northern Star*, has been the blight of democracy from the first moment he opened his mouth as its *professed advocate* . . . Not possessing a nature to appreciate intellectual exertions, he began his career by ridiculing our *'moral force humbuggery'* . . . By his constant appeals to the selfishness, vanity, and mere animal propensities of man, he succeeded in calling up a spirit of hate, intolerance and brute feeling, previously unknown among Reformers.

Source: William Lovett, *The life and struggles of William Lovett in pursuit of bread, knowledge and freedom*, London, 1876, pp. 294–97, Fitzroy edn, London, 1967, p. 245

3.2 Gammage on O'Connor

His broad massive forehead . . . bore evidence . . . of great intellectual force. To assert that he possessed a mind solid and steady was to say too much, no man with an equal amount of intellect was ever more erratic. Had the solidarity of his judgement been equal to his quickness of perception he would intellectually have been a great man, but this essential quality of greatness was lacked, hence his life presents a series of mistakes and contradictions . . . No man in the movement was so certain of popularity as

O'Connor. No man was so certain to lose it after its attainment. It was not until he proceeded to speak that the full extent of his influence was felt.

Source: R. C. Gammage, *The history of the Chartist movement, from its commencement down to the present times*, 2nd edn, Newcastle, 1894, p. 45

3.3 Adams on O'Connor

Next to this fault was the disposition [among the leaders] to quarrel. But quarrelling was almost inevitable when not one man but many men, desire to become dictators. It was almost equally inevitable when such a man as Feargus O'Connor, who had few of the qualities of a powerful leader save extraordinary force of character, had acquired absolute dominion over the cause . . . The common notion of O'Connor outside the ranks of his personal followers was that he was a charlatan and a humbug – an adventurer who traded on the passions of the people for his own profit and advantage. A correcter notion would have been that he was a victim of his own delusions.

Source: W. E. Adams, *Memoirs of a social atom*, London, 1903, pp. 203, 208–9

3.4 Cole on O'Connor

Feargus O'Connor was unquestionably the best-loved, as well as the most-hated, man in the Chartist movement. Not in one district alone, but all over England (much less, however, in either Wales or Scotland), he had an immense hold upon the people . . . Even amid the ruins of Chartism and the collapse of the Land Scheme in which many thousands had lost their money, O'Connor kept his popularity. When, after several years of confinement in a madhouse, he died in 1855, thousands followed his body to the grave, and there was mourning all over England for a lost leader.

The judgement of historians has differed markedly from the popular verdict. Hardly one historian of Chartism can write about O'Connor except in terms of acrimonious dislike. This is no doubt largely derived from the language used about him by his erstwhile colleagues, such as William Lovett, whose hatred of him comes out plainly in almost every reference. It is indeed abundantly clear that O'Connor was an impossible colleague . . . As an organiser and leader he was ruined by his incapacity for collaboration. He wanted to be boss; but he had no clear policy, especially at moments of crisis, when he said first one thing and then another, and always came down on what he felt likeliest to be the winning side. He was, in truth, a disastrous leader.

Source: G. D. H. Cole, *Chartist portraits*, London, 1941, pp. 300–01, 336

3.5 Epstein on O'Connor

O'Connor has often been severely criticised for having exerted an undemocratic, 'dictatorial' control over the Chartist movement. However, as David Jones has suggested, 'the problems which he faced deserve greater attention'. The central problem of national Chartist leadership was the maintenance of radical working-class unity. The magnitude of this task should not be forgotten. With remarkable forbearance, energy and enthusiasm O'Connor battled to overcome the divisions and sources of fragmentation within the working-class movement . . . In the early 1840s, the vulnerability of Chartism's national unity was tested. Both from outside and within the Chartist ranks the movement was faced with a series of 'rival' or alternative agitations . . . In spring 1841, O'Connor published his famous condemnation of 'Church Chartism, Teetotal Chartism, Knowledge Chartism and Household Suffrage Chartism' . . . Several weeks before the publication of this attack on the quadruple alliance of church, teetotal, knowledge and household-suffrage Chartism, O'Connor explained his position: 'I do not object to Chartists being religious – to Chartists being teetotal – to Chartists thirsting after knowledge, or to Chartists voting out of, and living in, their own houses'. His opposition was based rather upon his fears that these various tendencies might become splinter groups, dissipating the movement's strength.

Source: James Epstein, *The lion of freedom: Feargus O'Connor and the Chartist movement, 1832–1842*, London, 1982, pp. 236, 240

3.6 Thompson on O'Connor

By most of Chartism's historians, O'Connor has been seen as the evil genius of the movement. Only recently has this distortion begun to be redressed, but it is a judgement that will die hard. In fact, so far from being the exploiter and distorter of the Chartist movement, O'Connor was so much the centre of it that, had the name Chartist not be coined, the radical movement between 1838 and 1848 must surely have been called O'Connorite Radicalism. Remove him and his newspaper from the picture, and the movement fragments, localises and loses its continuity.

O'Connor was a politician rather than a theoretician. Throughout his career he held to certain principles, above all to the principles of universal (manhood) suffrage . . . But O'Connor retained his unquestioned leadership of the Chartist movement above all because he kept the matter of the suffrage in the forefront of his arguments. His political stance was simple . . . But, in the end, the qualities of leadership which keep a man at the head of a mass movement for ten years and more are not to be found in his political philosophy or his administrative ability alone. Too many historians have credited O'Connor with only the charismatic qualities of leadership, and it must be pointed out that he was a shrewd and capable politician and a not inconsiderable organiser and administrator in addition . . . No other leader or would-be leader in those days had the energy, ability, physique or charisma of Feargus O'Connor. For good or ill, he was the main inspiration and guiding force of the movement.

Source: Dorothy Thompson, *The Chartists: popular politics in the Industrial Revolution*, Aldershot, 1984, pp. 96–101

Document case-study questions

1 'He would say that, wouldn't he?' What conclusions did Lovett come to about O'Connor in 3.1? How can you account for these conclusions?

2 In what respects do 3.2 and 3.3 support the views expressed by Lovett in 3.1?

3 Why was O'Connor not a great leader according to the three contemporary sources (3.1, 3.2 and 3.3)?

4 How far does 3.4 support the views expressed in the three contemporary sources?

5 3.5 and 3.6 represent revisionist views of O'Connor. How do they attempt to rehabilitate him and his role within the Chartist movement?

6 Why have opinions of O'Connor been so polarised?

7 Contemporaries divided Chartists into 'physical- and moral-force' supporters. Historians of the movement accepted this division without real criticism. Why? What consequences has this had for our understanding of Chartism?

8 How should historians define the Chartist leadership?

Notes and references

1 John Saville, *1848: the British state and the Chartist movement*, Cambridge, 1987, pp. 200–05, provides a succinct commentary on historiographical developments and genres.

2 G. D. H. Cole, *Chartist portraits*, London, 1941, p. 30.

3 William Lovett, *The life and struggles of William Lovett in pursuit of bread, knowledge and freedom*, London, 1876, references to 1967 Fitzroy edition prefaced by R. H. Tawney, p. 75.

4 James Vernon, *Politics and the people: a study in English political culture, 1815–1867*, Cambridge, 1993, p. 251.

5 Vernon, *Politics and the people*, p. 253.

6 Christopher Hodgkinson, *The philosophy of leadership*, Oxford, 1983, is a valuable study of the principles underpinning leadership.

7 On Lovett, see Joyce M. Bellamy and John Saville (eds.), *Dictionary of labour history*, vol. 6, London, 1982; Joseph O. Baylen and Norbert J. Grossman (eds.), *Biographical dictionary of modern British radicals since 1770*, vol. 2 (1830–70), Brighton, 1984; and David Large, 'William Lovett', in P. Hollis (ed.), *Pressure from without in early Victorian England*, London, 1974, pp. 105–30. Joel Wiener, *William Lovett*, Manchester, 1989, is the best modern biography.

8 Theodore Rothstein, *From Chartism to labourism: historical sketches of the English working-class movement*, London, 1929.

9 Wiener, *William Lovett*, p. 139.

10 Wiener, *William Lovett*, pp. 1–3.

11 Lovett, *Life and struggles*, p. 174.

12 Lovett, *Life and struggles*, p. 210.

13 Thomas Cooper, *The life of Thomas Cooper*, 1872, reprinted with an introduction by John Saville, Leicester, 1971, p. 28.

14 Cole, *Chartist portraits*, p. 187.

15 Stephen Roberts' work on Cooper is the most recent and accurate: 'Thomas Cooper in Leicester, 1840–1843', *Transactions of the Leicestershire Archaeological and Historical Society*, vol. 61 (1987); 'Thomas Cooper: radical and poet, c. 1830–1860', *Bulletin of the Society for the Study of Labour History*, vol. 53 (1), (1988); 'The later radical career of Thomas Cooper, c. 1845–1855', *Transactions of the Leicestershire Archaeological and Historical Society*, vol. 64 (1990); and 'Thomas Cooper: a Victorian working-class writer', *Our History Journal*, vol. 16 (1990).

16 James Epstein, *The lion of freedom: Feargus O'Connor and the Chartist movement, 1832–1842*, London, 1982.

4 Chartism: phase 1, 1836–40

Chartism emerged from the maelstrom of radical activities that punctuated the mid-1830s. The campaigns against the unstamped press and the Poor Law Amendment Act, combined with opposition to establishment attacks on trade unions and the unsuccessful Ten Hour movement, created a climate of increasing suspicion and anxiety among the working classes. In many respects, the publication of the People's Charter in early 1838 marked the end of a process rather than a beginning: the 'six points' had already been widely discussed in London and in the provinces. The People's Charter, however, defined the mass platform and distinguished it from middle-class radical agitation.

Chartism before the Charter

In June 1836, the LWMA was formed with William Lovett as its secretary; Dorothy Thompson argues that it has 'in general been given more prominence as a precipitant of the Chartist movement than it deserves'.[1] Certainly, few of the characteristics of Chartism were to be found in the LWMA. Its members were little affected by Whig repression; they were definitely not particularly class-conscious; most were artisans; some may have been affected by competition from factories or sweated labour, but none were obvious casualties of industrial change. Membership cost one shilling per month and was further restricted to 'persons of good moral character among the industrious classes'. The LWMA's policy focused on education and moral reform, as well as the 'six points', and its favoured tactics – meetings, petitions and propaganda – were moderate and gradualist. It recognised that there were significant differences between the interests of the working class and those of other classes, but exhibited none of the strident opposition to class co-operation that later distinguished some areas of Chartism. In many respects, the LWMA was therefore a conservative organisation.

In February 1837, the LWMA held a public meeting at the Crown and Anchor public house in the Strand to discuss the petitioning of parliament for what eventually emerged as the 'six points'. Meetings on 31 May and 7 June between working men and the 'liberal members of parliament' led to the formation of a committee of six drawn from each group – and later, probably in December, limited to Lovett and J. A. Roebuck alone – which was then appointed to draw up a parliamentary bill incorporating the Crown and Anchor petition. When Roebuck withdrew, following his defeat at Bath in the 1837 election, it was

Francis Place who did the drafting. The charter that emerged – a very moderate document that restated the traditional radical demand for universal suffrage – was essentially the work of Lovett and Place, although suggestions from the committee of twelve and from the LWMA led to revisions of the original document.

Despite its role in creating the petition, at no time did the LWMA have a monopoly of London working-class radicalism. In September 1835, O'Connor had founded his Great Radical Association, which was amalgamated with the Marylebone Radical Association in December. At least eight other associations were formed in different parts of London between 1835 and 1836, although none lasted for long.[2] The Great Radical Association was particularly important to O'Connor, for it marked the effective beginnings of his political career in England and acted as a springboard for his rapid emergence as a national Chartist leader. The first real challenge to the LWMA came from the Central National Association, which existed for only a few months in early 1837, which provided a platform for a blistering attack by O'Brien[3] on the LWMA as 'tools of the Malthusian sham-radicals'. More formidable, in the longer term, was the East London Democratic Association, which was set up by the young George Julian Harney[4] in January 1837. This organisation became increasingly class-conscious and less moderate; it sought support from working men of every kind and attacked the LWMA for its elitism and caution. The uneasy relationship between the different associations broke down in early 1838. Lovett attacked O'Connor as 'the great "I AM" of politics' and Harney, among others, resigned from the LWMA. On 10 August the East London Democratic Association was formally reorganised as the London Democratic Association.[5]

Birmingham was the other main centre that was significant in the emergence of Chartism.[6] The Birmingham Political Union (BPU) had played an important part in the reform agitation between 1830 and 1832 and was successfully revived in April and May 1837. A meeting at Newhall Hill on 19 June was attended by between 15,000 and 150,000 people (the total depending on the prejudice of the observer). Here Thomas Attwood, the leader of the BPU, threatened to produce 2 million men, banded together in a 'sacred and solemn compact', and then went on to say that, if their demands for political reform were ignored, there might be a general strike of both masters and men for an entire week. The following month, the BPU ignored a request from the LWMA for co-operation in seeking universal suffrage; it took several months before the BPU would promote the cause of democracy. The initial tactic of the BPU was to appeal directly to the Whig government. Melbourne, the prime minister, may have been impressed by a deputation from the union in late June 1837, but did nothing, and the country as a whole paid little attention to it. The BPU's membership declined rapidly, from 8,800 in the late summer of 1837 to around 3,000 by the end of the year; moderate reform did not attract either the attention or support that the union needed. By October, even Attwood had conceded that the only viable strategy was universal suffrage. In December 1837 the union therefore addressed the nation and proclaimed its intention to seek universal suffrage as 'a rightful inheritance'. In addition, the need for co-operation with other radical groups was accepted. As Carlos Flick, the modern historian of the BPU, states: 'The council was prepared to advocate, not ancient principles belonging to the people as a matter of historical right, but rather the claims of a single class, supported as a matter of political expediency.'[7] On 11 December the LWMA applauded the conversion of the BPU to democracy and the following day Henry Hetherington[8] visited Birmingham on behalf of the LWMA.

The BPU was less exclusively artisan than the LWMA, drawing as it did on support from both the middle classes and the unskilled. Attwood[9] was particularly interested in proposals to stimulate the economy by means of currency reform, though these took second place to universal suffrage after late 1837. Yet in other respects the two organisations were similar; the problem was that both had become political anachronisms. Political unions of the Birmingham type that appealed for class co-operation did not have the same attraction in 1837 and 1838 that they had had between 1830 and 1832. The middle classes were increasingly unwilling to support working-class demands for reform and those political unions that did emerge in 1837 and 1838 were modelled on the LWMA, with few middle-class members. Like the LWMA, they were elitist and spoke for only a small proportion of the working classes. Both the BPU and the LWMA were inexorably sidelined by the more assertive approach and national appeal of O'Connor.

Bringing the movement together: an inauspicious beginning

The People's Charter was finally published in May 1838, and was adopted by the existing network of radical organisations. Historians have tended to date the start of the movement from the first public unveiling of Chartist demands, and most writers have followed Francis Place in giving the precedence in terms of time to the People's Charter over the National Petition. In fact, these two core documents of the Chartist movement were produced at about the same time. Its basic programme – the Charter – derived unquestionably from the LWMA, but it was the BPU that proposed not only a national petition but also, as Thompson says, 'more significant in terms of political action', the calling of a general Chartist convention.

The initial problem was that the National Petition and the People's Charter were so similar that the BPU and LWMA seemed to be getting in each other's way. It became increasingly clear that the only way in which to get the movement under way in England was for the different radical groups to co-operate. The LWMA would therefore rouse southern England, leaving Birmingham responsible for the Midlands. The difficulty created by the rival documents was sensibly resolved, and the BPU and LWMA each agreed to approve the other's document. It was, however, Feargus O'Connor who became the 'key' player. His followers began to set up rival 'democratic associations', calling for more aggressive tactics and a broader programme of change, including the repeal of the Poor Law. Many working-class associations began to ally with them, rather than with Lovett's moderate LWMA. By mid-1838, O'Connor was exercising considerable power over northern popular radicalism through his newspaper the *Northern Star*,[10] founded in November 1837, as well as by bringing the radical groups together in the Leeds-based Great Northern Union in April 1838.[11] This union is often seen as an association that was developed by O'Connor to offset the influence of Lovett and the LWMA in the north; in fact, it was a means of redirecting the forces of the anti-Poor Law movement, which were on the wane, into the emerging Chartist movement. The union was a loose federation of local radical associations, lasted only a short time, and was never a particularly effective centralised organisation. But it did serve the purposes of both building up O'Connor's leadership in the north and welding the northern radicals into one body. However, O'Connor recognised that he could not ignore either the BPU or the LWMA and, by early June 1838, was stating his initial willingness to co-operate with the Birmingham reformers.

Co-operation between the BPU, the LWMA and the Great Northern Union made good tactical sense: local action was simply not going to work because it was too fragmented. Regional action, on the other hand, provided a new pattern of agitation through co-operation between the different organisations arguing for democracy. This approach may have been politically sound, but there were major ideological and organisational obstacles to effective co-operation. The LWMA saw political education as the key to eventual success, while the BPU had already stated that it sought to achieve its objectives peacefully. O'Connor appealed directly to the growing class-consciousness, however, and behind his fighting words lurked the threat of 'ulterior sanctions'.

From August 1838, a series of regional meetings were held to elect delegates to the national Chartist Convention that was scheduled to be held early in 1839 in London. The eight Birmingham delegates were elected at a meeting on 6 August, for example; the numbers which attended it fell somewhere between the 20,000 estimated by the conservative press and the inflated figure of 300,000 put forward in the *Northern Star*. Here Attwood renewed his proposal for a 'sacred week' of idleness from work if the petition was rejected. The London meeting on 17 September was, by comparison, poorly attended – a mere 15,000 were in the audience. O'Connor held a meeting at Kersal Moor near Manchester (attended by 200,000 people) on 24 September; at Liverpool the following day (attended by a dismal maximum of 5,000 people); and in the West Riding at Hartshead Moor (with an audience of an estimated 250,000 people) on 15 October. The national pattern of meetings to elect delegates was patchy. In the Midlands, for example, neighbouring towns failed to send representatives to the Birmingham demonstration; Tory opponents prevented meetings at Kidderminster and Wolverhampton, and rioting was narrowly avoided; meetings at Coventry, Stratford-on-Avon and Nuneaton were poorly attended. When the Chartist Convention met in early 1839, the regions comprising Warwickshire outside Birmingham, Worcestershire and all of Staffordshire south of the Potteries contributed fewer than 20,000 signatures to the National Petition. The delicate alliance of the three groups of reformers was beginning to unravel.

O'Connor became increasingly frustrated with the activities of both the BPU and the LWMA.[12] In fact, he generally ignored them, naming his allies instead as the 'men of Birmingham' and 'the London operatives'. After the end of August 1838, no members of the BPU attended meetings in the Midlands. In London, the LWMA's focus on the People's Charter to the exclusion of the petition was a source of grievance to the BPU – only 19,000 signatures on the petition came from London, and the rest of the south and south-west added only a further 7,245. Only their mutual suspicion of O'Connor kept them allied. For his part, O'Connor made little reference to the Charter in his speeches other than vaguely acknowledging its principles. The National Petition, however, warranted his full attention. He was not, however, favourably disposed to the BPU's notion, first proposed in August, of a 'national rent' to support the work of the Chartist Convention when it met. Indeed, he simply ignored it and this is reflected in the failure of Newcastle, Manchester and the West Riding to make any collection whatsoever. Lovett, too, had his suspicions regarding the levy, and London had only contributed £15 by the time the convention met. These difficulties might have been tolerable had O'Connor kept to his own territory, but he did not. This irritated both organisations, but all O'Connor did was to complain of the 'base and sneaking opposition by which he had been formerly cramped in his exertions'. The choice of delegates to the convention also exposed increasingly irreconcilable differences within Chartism and marked a crucial turning point in the movement. There was no objection from the BPU and LWMA as long as the delegates were moderate, and BPU council members were chosen as the delegates for Birmingham while, in London, most delegates came from the LWMA. It became increasingly clear, however, that there would be a significant number of O'Connorites at the convention.

The growing unease of the BPU and the LWMA was made worse by the need to decide what to do if parliament rejected the petition. Attwood's proposal for a general strike was based on the very unlikely assumption that masters would back their workers and would continue to pay their wages. Lovett wanted to renew the petitioning effort over and over again so that, at least in theory, parliament would have to pass the People's Charter in order to stop the process. O'Connor bragged that he would have 500,000 men deliver the petition to parliament, but failed to answer the question of what should be done if it was rejected. None of these constitutional approaches seemed likely to work, so what of unconstitutional action? Each of the three parties knew that actual, as opposed to threatened, violence would be counter-productive. The issue was how far the radicals should go in raising the threat and fear of violence without having to put it into practice. O'Connor's supporters seemed to welcome the prospect of violence as long as it was spontaneous and did not implicate them, but the BPU and LWMA did not want to risk any bloodshed at all. Between November 1838 and early 1839, O'Connor found himself under attack in Birmingham, London, and also in Scotland, from those whom he called 'moral cowards', who condemned physical force; he was able to see them off, however.

What was O'Connor's attitude to physical force in late 1838? Was it all a bluff? He never admitted to having advised the use of violence.[13] He argued that he had pointed out the physical reality behind moral force, a reality that he neither created nor controlled. He borrowed heavily from the eighteenth-century tradition that there was an established constitutional right of armed resistance to tyranny. The Chartists were therefore acting in defence of the constitution, he maintained, rather than seeking to destroy it. O'Connor may have avoided directly recommending violence, but he made few objections to those, like Joseph Rayner Stephens,[14] who did. His speeches were deliberately ambiguous but, as James Epstein says, 'ambiguity was inherent to platform agitation'. He thereby successfully trod the line between legality and sedition, and between moderation and revolutionary fervour, with innate skill.

This struggle within Chartism can be seen in the movement's rapidly growing press. The Chartist press was one of the foundations on which the movement was built. Many of the leading Chartist journalists – people like John Cleave, Henry Hetherington and William Benbow[15] – as well as such platform orators as George Julian Harney, had gained their initial experience during the 'war of the unstamped' in the first half of the 1830s. From January 1839 to March 1840, the LWMA published *The Charter* to put forward its position, while the London Democratic Association produced the *London Democrat*. In Scotland, moral force found support in the *Ayrshire Examiner*, but in the press war O'Connor undoubtedly had the strongest weapon at his disposal in the *Northern Star*.

The Chartist Convention, 1839

The Chartist Convention[16] finally met in London on 4 February 1839.[17] The idea of a convention was nothing new in 1839: British parliamentary reforming movements had been regularly organised round the idea of an alternative or anti parliament since the 1750s.[18] Most radicals viewed the convention as a means of seeing the petition through parliament. Yet the convention challenged the unrepresentative character of the House of Commons, and questioned the legitimacy of the existing suffrage simply because the convention itself had been elected by universal male suffrage. Throughout the country, Chartists therefore regarded the convention as an alternative, more legitimate, government, to which they gave their loyalty.

The convention's delegates

In many respects, the convention was rather less representative than O'Connor claimed: under half of the delegates were working men. Of the eight elected Birmingham delegates, for example, only one (John Collins) came from the working class. Middle-class radicals like Peter Bussey of Bradford and John Frost of Newport were in the majority, however, having a degree of financial independence that working men were denied. Indeed, never again would Chartism have such a wide range of middle-class leadership. Thus it was that the convention had the appearance of middle-class 'respectability'. Furthermore, not only was it initially not a primarily working-class assembly, but certain areas were better represented than others. A quarter of the delegates, for instance, lived in London. The LWMA, a relatively small radical association, manipulated the election of eight delegates at the expense of the various metropolitan districts and other radical groups. When O'Connor later claimed that the LWMA had tried to 'fix' the membership of the convention, he was not far from the truth.

O'Connor's role in the convention

Lovett's later analysis suggested that O'Connor sought to control the convention from the outset. In fact, while no other leader rivalled his influence within the convention, he carefully avoided forming a 'party'. Indeed, O'Connor often acted as mediator between the delegates of the convention and the rank-and-file members. For him, the issue was maintaining working-class belief in the convention as the main agency of Chartist leadership and action. At no other time had Chartism captured such a wide degree of working-class support and O'Connor did not want to see that support dissipated.[19]

The status of the convention

Uncertainty about the status of the convention existed from the start. The National Petition had been signed by only about 500,000 people by February 1839, and many people believed that it should be a more substantial document before being presented to parliament. An early debate suggested that 'missionaries' should be sent round the country in order to drum up more signatures (this, in fact, occurred during the summer of 1839). But, as one of the BPU delegates asked, was this the function of the convention? Many delegates were rooted in their own localities and were highly suspicious of 'outsiders' with no local interests stirring up their people. There was also a question mark over the convention's legality. The central problem of what should be done if the petition was rejected remained. O'Connor argued forcefully for an early resolution of this problem so that both the movement and the government knew what the result of any rejection would be, believing that this would force concessions from the Whigs. Most delegates were, however, opposed to a premature discussion of any 'ulterior sanctions'. This position left the convention in an ambiguous position and weakened whatever tactical advantage it had. The petition was therefore delayed, not being presented to parliament until June and not being rejected till mid-July 1839. Failure to resolve the issue of 'ulterior sanctions' meant that the movement had lost valuable months in preparing a plan of alternative action.

As the language of militants like Harney became more extreme, many of the convention's moderate members – principally those from Scotland and Birmingham – returned home. The Birmingham delegates resigned on 28 March 1839 and defections continued throughout April and May, primarily from the ranks of the middle-class delegates. Their replacements came from the working class. O'Connor's role became even more crucial as he appeared to stand above the convention's in-fighting. His concern was that the convention might degenerate into sectional activities and that this would threaten the unity of the movement. By the end of April it was apparent that the movement needed more decisive leadership, which prompted O'Connor's campaign to move the convention out of London. When Melbourne's government resigned,[20] the National Petition could not be presented, and the remaining 35 delegates moved to Birmingham on 13 May 1839.

Once established in Birmingham, the convention finally issued its manifesto. This was its most specific outcome, and it recommended certain ulterior measures to be put to the Chartist rank and file at simultaneous meetings to be held during Whit week in late May. In addition, proposals for a 'sacred month', or general strike, were put forward. The convention then adjourned until 1 July 1839 to await the outcome of the local meetings. The resolution to allow these decisions to be made at the local level represented a further weakening of its leadership by the convention.

The government's response

Both the convention and the Chartist leadership now found themselves under increasing pressure from hardening government attitudes.[21] Lord John Russell, the home secretary, initially resisted those demanding repressive action, but by mid-1839 a firmer and more confident government policy emerged: drilling of men was banned; lord lieutenants were given powers to raise and arm special constables; and 6,000 troops were stationed in the north under General Napier. In addition, Henry Vincent had been arrested for sedition in late April, and two other leaders had also been detained before the convention moved to Birmingham. The Metropolitan Police put down rioting Chartists at Llanidloes in Montgomeryshire, central Wales, in May. There were Chartist arrests in Wiltshire. In south Lancashire, Chartists were arrested for drilling, and 13 Chartists were seized in a police raid on the London Democratic Association headquarters. In mid-June, in response to the growing number of arrests and anticipating more to come, O'Connor set up the National Defence Fund to support the defence costs of those in detention. But no attempt was made to arrest the convention's delegates en masse, or to declare its sittings illegal: the government was sufficiently astute not to precipitate a crisis that the Chartists could exploit.

Was a successful Chartist insurrection likely in the summer of 1839? O'Connor and other Chartist leaders (rightly) recognised that it would have stood little chance of success, for there was no evidence that the army would have supported a rising. For its part, the government avoided any flagrant attack on popular liberties, like that at Peterloo 20 years earlier, that could have given the initiative to the Chartists. The Chartists' mass meetings therefore passed without any violent confrontation and, when the convention reconvened in early July, it was still faced with the question of 'ulterior sanctions', and especially the role of the 'sacred month'. For most Chartist leaders, such a national holiday was not seen as a peaceful tactic. R. J. Richardson, for example, believed that a 'sacred month' would 'be a great revolution in the country', while Harney, with characteristic bravura, insisted that 'a national holiday would be nothing more or less than a civil war'. Yet even William Lovett found himself supporting the notion of a 'sacred month' as 'the only effectual remedy for the sufferings of the people'. A final decision on the date of the 'sacred month' was delayed until after parliament voted on the Charter, but clearly the convention had finally taken a distinct step towards revolutionary action.

The rejection of the petition

On 4 July 1839, the day after the convention had taken its decision on 'ulterior sanctions', the Birmingham authorities brought in police from London. Their violent action at a peaceful Chartist meeting in the Bull Ring ended in riots. The military was called in when the police found themselves under attack and O'Connor saw this as a vindication of his stance that soldiers would not side with the working class. Its effect was, however, to harden the Chartist resolve and to strengthen support for the 'sacred month'. The convention, reduced in size by resignations, differences of opinion and now arrests, moved back to London. On 12 July, the House of Commons rejected the petition by 235 votes to 46. The convention had finally to face up to the issues of violence and resistance.

It was the absence of clear leadership in July and August 1839 on O'Connor's part that proved decisive. Until then, he had provided a consistent lead over the question of 'ulterior' measures in the convention. Government repression, the rejection of the petition, and the convention's decision to call a 'sacred month' on 17 July, led many Chartists to expect some form of decisive confrontation. O'Connor, however, concluded that the movement was unprepared for such a confrontation with government and sought to prevent its ultimate success being jeopardised by an abortive or partial general strike. On 17 July, the convention had voted, by 13 to 6, to hold a 'sacred month', despite letters from local associations questioning the wisdom of calling a general strike during a severe trade depression. On 24 July, however, following consultations with 63 Welsh, Scottish and English associations that showed support from only 9, and knowing of O'Connor's opposition, the convention reversed the decision. This represented a deliberate drawing back by the Chartist leadership, especially on the part of O'Brien and O'Connor, from direct confrontation with government. It left the movement without an effective strategy, however, and led to the dissolution of the convention on 6 September. A truncated national holiday was, in fact, held for three days during August 1839, but its importance mainly lay in the opportunity that it gave the government to arrest local Chartist leaders in considerable numbers.

It is easy to write the convention off as a complete failure. Its divisions, its inability to provide consistent leadership and its failure to develop an effective strategy with which to carry through universal suffrage demonstrated the ineffectiveness of the Chartist movement. Yet the convention lasted for seven months in the face of intense opposition from government and hostility from the other classes of society; it was elected on democratic principles; and it was financed through the efforts of working people. It was based on the defence of established constitutional principles and demonstrated the ability of the working class to develop and maintain alternative political institutions. Despite the rank-and-file criticism of his changing attitudes, O'Connor still had the confidence of most Chartists.

The Newport Rising, 1839

The move towards direct action

By the autumn of 1839, most of the Chartist leaders were either in prison or on bail awaiting trial. The *Northern Star* spoke of a 'reign of terror' but, in many respects, the government dealt leniently with the many Chartists who had been arrested. Most were given the option of pleading guilty to the charges against them, and were then bound over to keep the peace – normally for two years – before being allowed to go home. This option was not offered to those who were seen as ringleaders, or who had been arrested carrying firearms. The number eventually tried and imprisoned – perhaps 200 – was small, given the size of the protests that had taken place. Joseph Rayner Stephens, who had been arrested in December 1838, came up for trial at Chester in August 1839 and was imprisoned for 18 months; Lovett and Collins were also tried in August and received a year's imprisonment, the same as Henry Vincent. Some Chartists were brought to trial in the autumn, but others had to wait until the spring or summer of 1840.

Until the summer of 1839, Chartism was marked by both its openness and its emphasis on constitutional types of agitation and organisation. The failure by the Chartist leadership to provide a clear national strategy saw the initiative move to local associations. Growing frustration with the attitude of the government led to a revival of the conspiratorial tradition of direct action and armed force. O'Connor had always opposed this sort of action, arguing that united national action could only be satisfied by open constitutional procedures. He sought to redirect the movement by emphasising the need for reorganisation and the necessity of a social programme to accompany the demands for universal suffrage. How much O'Connor knew about the secret plotting is difficult to judge: he was in Ireland from 5 October to 2 November 1839. His reasons for going to Ireland, given almost four years later – that, facing prison, he wanted to see friends and put his affairs in order – are not entirely convincing. A more plausible explanation is the difficulty he faced in giving the movement direction. Whatever the explanation may be, his absence was eminently convenient. James Epstein commented that this 'stands out as the only period during a long career of radical leadership when O'Connor appears to have voluntarily removed himself from the centre of national agitation'.[22] There is also some evidence to suggest that O'Connor was deliberately left in the dark.

Whether or not O'Connor knew about the plans for direct action, he cannot escape some responsibility for creating the atmosphere in which they developed. While his commitment to open national protest must be stressed, his position on defensive arming was fundamentally ambiguous. Successful revolution requires effective co-ordination, nationwide organisation and efficient communication

The Newport Rising. After the rejection of the Chartist Petition in 1839, the 'physical force' Chartists called for violent action. This contemporary illustration shows a crowd attacking the Westgate Hotel in Newport, south Wales.

and, in 1839, as the abortive risings demonstrated, this was clearly not the case. Instead, O'Connor asserted the need for another convention: a few days after the Newport Rising he wrote in the *Northern Star*: 'for if we looked at the occurrences of the day, we see that it is only organised bodies that can act with effect'.

The Newport Rising

The risings were largely community responses. There was unquestionably an extensive underground network linking the north-east, Yorkshire, Lancashire, Nottinghamshire, Birmingham, Wales and London, and this continued to exist after the Welsh rising in Newport. Whether there was a widespread plan for a national rising was, as Dorothy Thompson asserts, 'unlikely'. In the event, only south Wales rose. Had the rising been successful it might, Thompson suggests, have acted as 'the inspiration for similar acts in other parts of the country rather than to form the first of a series of inter-connected risings that had already been planned'.[23] On the night of 3–4 November 1839, 7,000 miners and iron-workers from the south Wales coalfield marched in three columns to Newport with the aim of releasing Henry Vincent[24] from Newport jail.[25] There is also evidence that they intended to launch a massive uprising to create a people's republic in the Welsh valleys which, they hoped, would spread to other parts of Britain. Troops opened fire, killing at least 22 and wounding another 50; the rest fled in confusion and many, including leaders[26] like John Frost, Zephaniah Williams and Charles Jones, were arrested during the succeeding days, when over 250 people were arraigned in the last mass-treason trial in British history. Death sentences were passed on the three leaders, although these were later commuted to transportation to Australia for life. The Newport Rising was not a small-scale affair, or the work of Whig *agents provocateurs*, or even simply a 'monster demonstration', as earlier historians concluded, but was the product of a radical political culture in an area where class divisions were clearly defined.

The aftermath of the Newport Rising

Ironically, the Welsh rising reopened the constitutional debate. The failure at Newport and the arrest of the Welsh leaders gave O'Connor a cause around which to rebuild the national movement. He received considerable support in this from Dr John Taylor, a leading Chartist who had been deeply involved in the plans for revolution and who remained profoundly committed to this confrontational approach. Yet again, however, there was a difference of emphasis. O'Connor viewed the next Chartist convention, which in the event only met for three weeks, as a means of creating a permanent Chartist organisation, while Taylor, as well as many local militants, wanted it to act as a co-ordinating body for revolution. The delegates to the convention were local militants who, unlike the delegates to the first convention, were strictly accountable to the local movement. In the end, O'Connor did not attend the London convention, despite being elected as the delegate for Dewsbury, and his relationship to it was, to say the least, ambiguous. In late December 1839, a deputation met O'Connor to ask why he had not attended the convention and what his attitude would be if Frost were convicted. The radical William Ashton later reported that O'Connor had said that if this happened 'he would place himself at the head of the people of England, and have a b----y r----n to save them'. O'Connor's version was different: 'I would rather risk my life than allow Frost to be hung [sic].'[27] The convention itself was concerned with raising money for Frost's defence and with petitioning the queen (Victoria), but plans were also made for revolution.

Whatever was planned, and abortive insurrections[28] did take place in Sheffield, Dewsbury and Bradford[29] in January 1840, O'Connor, through the medium of the *Northern Star*, made it clear in an editorial on 11 January 1840 that he opposed the whole plan for insurrection. Frost was convicted and O'Connor – probably correctly – recognised that peaceful action was the only means of saving him from the gallows. Although the Whig cabinet decided on 29 January that Frost, Williams and Jones should be executed as an example to the country, three days later their sentences were commuted to transportation for life. This was an astute move which defused a potentially dangerous situation. It also deeply affected the Chartists' attitude to government: it seemed to demonstrate that a peaceful campaign could work, and also called into question the long-held working-class belief in the fundamental violence of government. It additionally marked the end of the first phase of Chartist protest.

In February 1840, the movement demonstrated its self-confidence, mass support and energy in the petition campaign in support of the Welsh leaders. Yet in the weeks leading up to O'Connor's own conviction for sedition and imprisonment in May 1840, the mass platform evaporated; delegate meetings held in March and April at Manchester and Nottingham were poorly attended. Increasingly, however, most Chartist localities came round to O'Connor's position: that reorganisation, not revolution, was what was needed. In many localities, this recognition had already begun by the spring of 1840. The tone of the movement was beginning to change: it lost some of its early spontaneity and optimism and its belief that the acceptance of the Charter was imminent. Unlike earlier radical movements, however, Chartism did not collapse: instead it reformed itself, and by the time that O'Connor was released from York Castle in September 1841, the foundations for a working-class political party had been laid.

Document case study
The Newport Rising

The Newport Rising of November 1839 in Wales was one of the most dramatic episodes of the Chartist movement; it is also one of the most contested. Was it merely a local disturbance bereft of any national significance, or did it mark the beginnings of a British revolution? Contemporaries were divided on the issue and, until recently, the view of orthodox historians was that it represented a 'monster demonstration' that went disastrously wrong. This view has come in for some vigorous criticism from revisionist writers, especially from David Jones.

4.1 A Chartist view

At least eight thousand men, mostly miners employed in the neighbourhood (which is very densely populated) were engaged in the attack upon the town of Newport and . . . many of them were armed . . . The ultimate design of the leaders does not appear; but it probably was to rear the standard of rebellion throughout Wales, in hopes of being able to hold the royal forces at bay, in that mountainous district, until the people of England, assured by successes, should rise en masse, for the same objects. According to the evidence now before the world, Mr Frost, the late member of the Convention, led the rioters, and he, with others, has been committed for high treason. On entering Newport, the people marched straight to the Westgate Hotel, where the magistrates, with about 40 soldiers were assembled, being fully apprised of the intended outbreak. The Riot Act was read, and the soldiers fired down, with ease and security, upon the people who had first broken and fired into the windows . . . About thirty of the people are known to have been killed, and several to have been wounded.

Source: *The Charter*, 17 November 1839

4.2 A Welsh clergyman's view

One very prominent fault of our working men is their readiness to allow themselves to be made the dupes of cunning and designing men . . . The Chartist movement of the year 1839 originated in a similar manner. A number of mob orators came down from England, who, by their thundering declamation against the oppression and injustice of the aristocracy, and fair promises of a perfect earthly paradise to the working classes as soon as the points of the charter would become the law of the land, soon gathered around their standards hundreds of confident expectants of the best things on earth. But, in the course of a few months all their high expectations ended in a disgraceful riot, poverty, imprisonment and death.

Source: Thomas Rees, 'The working classes of Wales', in *Miscellaneous papers on subjects relating to Wales*, London, 1867, p. 19

4.3 Lovett on Newport (or is it just another attack on O'Connor?)

Of the cause of this unhappy affair I had no opportunity of learning while in prison; but soon after I came out I made enquiries, and from a person who took an active part in matters pertaining to it, I learnt the following: – That the chief cause that led to the outbreak was the treatment pursued towards Vincent in particular, as well as of the Chartists generally. No sooner, however, did he [O'Connor] find out that they were so far in earnest as described, that he set about to render the outbreak ineffectual; notwithstanding all his previous incitements to arming and preparedness, and all his boast and swaggering at public meetings, and in the columns of the *Star*, he is said to have engaged George White to go into Yorkshire and Lancashire to assure the people that no rising would take place in Wales; and Charles Jones was sent into Wales, to assure the Welsh that there would be no rising in Yorkshire and that it had all been a Government plot . . . Fergus [*sic*], apprehensive of being called upon to set an heroic example, in those rising times, thought it a timely opportunity for visiting Ireland, so that by the time he came back most of the foolish outbreaks were over.

Source: William Lovett, *The life and struggles of William Lovett in pursuit of bread, knowledge and freedom*, London, 1876, Fitzroy edn, London, 1967, pp. 197–99

4.4 A Fabian perspective

The 'Newport Rising' was a small affair; and its leader was a small man, not only in stature, but in importance too. If Frost had not been the leading figure in the 'Rising', there would have been little to make him more memorable than many other local protagonists of Chartism whose names are now forgotten . . . But there was not much 'to' him; and even martyrdom did not make him look like a great man . . . Was there a plan for a national Chartist uprising after the rejection of the National Petition of 1839, and, if so, was Frost privy to it, or even one of its chief instigators? Did the colliers and ironworkers who marched on Newport during the night of November 3, 1839, believe that they were the advance guard of the British Revolution; and, if so, who was responsible for making them hold this belief? If there was a national plan, why did nothing happen in Lancashire or Yorkshire, where the main strength of the Chartists lay? . . . I have done what I can to answer these questions; but some are unanswerable, despite the efforts of historical students to sift out the truth. Probably some of them will remain without answers that can be proved correct.

Source: G. D. H. Cole, *Chartist portraits*, London, 1941, pp. 159–60

4.5 David Williams, writing in 1939

It may be that the planning of an insurrection, even of a local character, existed only in the minds of the authorities, that there was scarcely any planning, and that the affair was suddenly decided upon only a few days before it took place. Yet it has to be admitted that it is very difficult to reconstruct the activities of the Chartist leaders during the month of October, whether they were intentionally keeping their movements secret or not.

Source: David Williams, *John Frost: a study in Chartism*, Cardiff, 1939, reprinted New York, 1969, pp. 196–97

4.6 Newport revisited after 20 years

The Chartists elsewhere were, no doubt, threatening to rise, but there is no evidence that the Newport rising was to be a signal for a general rising. Nor is there much sense in believing that the Chartists intended to 'seize' Newport. The three contingents could so easily have entered the town from three directions, and, if necessary, destroyed the bridge to stop the mail, but they were at pains to join forces outside the town, at the expense of bringing the Pontypool men considerably out of their way, and they entered the town from the other side. This would confirm the belief that their purpose was a mass demonstration; as a plan to capture the town it is patently absurd. Equally absurd is the theory that their purpose was to liberate Vincent. There had been much talk of doing this . . . But Vincent was imprisoned in Monmouth; if the Chartists thought to liberate him they would not have brought the Pontypool men down to Newport, then making them almost retrace their steps to Usk before proceeding an equal distance in the opposite direction to Monmouth. The only reasonable explanation of the Newport riot is that it was intended as a monster demonstration.

Source: David Williams, 'Chartism in Wales', in Asa Briggs (ed.), *Chartist studies*, London, 1959, p. 241

4.7 A revisionist view

The nature of the rising was formed by the environment, geographical and ideological, that was industrial South Wales. The idea of a people's army from the hills descending on established towns and fortifying them was not new in Welsh history . . . Xenophobic English newspaper correspondents later suggested that such a rising 'on the hills' was nothing less than a nationalist rebellion and some talked, rather inconsistently, of Vincent being crowned 'King' of a self-contained Welsh republic. It seems improbable, however, that the industrial workmen thought in terms of a nationalist revolt; they hoped to control and fortify an area, and, whilst waiting for other clashes between soldiers and the population, set up a provisional Chartist 'Executive Government of England', with Frost as its President . . . The special nature of Welsh industrial society and Welsh Chartism helped to bring about a revolutionary situation on this side of the border, but, as Thomas Phillips in his defence of Wales later remarked, the local rising was originally conceived as part of a general insurrection.

Source: David J. V. Jones, *The last rising: the Newport insurrection of 1839*, Oxford, 1985, pp. 208–9

Document case-study questions

1 What were the main motives for the march on Newport according to 4.1?

2 In what ways does Thomas Rees, in 4.2, provide an alternative explanation?

3 Compare the explanation for the rising in 4.3 with those in 4.1 and 4.2.

4 4.2 and 4.3 were written with the advantage of hindsight. Only 4.1 provides a contemporary explanation. Does this matter? Explain your answer.

5 G. D. H. Cole provides further explanations for the Newport Rising in 4.4. In what respects do these help or hinder your analysis of 4.1, 4.2 and 4.3?

6 In what respects did David Williams' view of the Newport Rising remain the same between 1939 (4.5) and 1959 (4.6)?

7 David Jones provides a revolutionary explanation for the Newport Rising in 4.7. On what does he base his conclusion?

8 'The Newport Rising: "a small affair", "a monster demonstration", "a failed revolution"?' Discuss.

Notes and references

1 Dorothy Thompson, *The Chartists: popular politics in the Industrial Revolution*, Aldershot, 1984, p. 57.

2 On O'Connor's development as a radical during the mid-1830s, see James Epstein, *The lion of freedom: Feargus O'Connor and the Chartist movement, 1832–1842*, London, 1982, pp. 24–31.

3 Alfred Plummer, *Bronterre: a political biography of Bronterre O'Brien, 1804–1864*, London, 1971, is the standard work on this enigmatic figure. Joseph O. Baylen and Norbert J. Grossman (eds.), *Biographical dictionary of modern British radicals since 1770*, vol. 2 (1830–1870), Brighton, 1984, is a useful shorter study.

4 A. R. Schoyen, *The Chartist challenge: a portrait of George Julian Harney*, London, 1958, remains the best biography.

5 On this, see Jennifer Bennett, 'The London Democratic Association, 1837–41: a study in London radicalism', in James Epstein and Dorothy Thompson (eds.), *The Chartist experience: studies in working-class radicalism and culture, 1830–1860*, London, 1982, pp. 87–119.

6 Carlos Flick, *The Birmingham Political Union and the movements for reform in Britain, 1830–1839*, Folkestone, 1978, provides a sound analysis.

7 Flick, *The Birmingham Political Union*, pp. 123–24.

8 Ambrose G. Barker, *Henry Hetherington, 1792–1849*, London, 1938, remains the only modern biography. Baylen and Grossman (eds.), *Biographical dictionary*, provides a shorter, more recent, alternative.

9 David J. Moss, *Thomas Attwood: the biography of a radical*, Montreal, 1990, pp. 262–87, deals with what the author calls Attwood's 'failure' in 1838 and early 1839.

10 The creation of the *Northern Star* is dealt with most effectively in Epstein, *The lion of freedom*, pp. 60–89. Thompson, *The Chartists*, pp. 37–56, places it in the context of the burgeoning Chartist press.

11 On the emergence of O'Connor as the central figure within Chartism with the formation of the Great Northern Union, see Epstein, *The lion of freedom*, pp. 90–108.

12 On O'Connor's relationship with the BPU, Epstein, *The lion of freedom*, pp. 108–10 is the most succinct analysis.

13 The ambiguity of O'Connor's position is explored in Epstein, *The lion of freedom*, pp. 116–37.

14 Michael S. Edwards, *Purge this realm: a life of Joseph Rayner Stephens*, London, 1994, pp. 38–106, deals with Stephens' 'Chartist years'.

15 Biographies of Cleave and Benbow can be found in J. Bellamy and J. Saville (ed.), *Dictionary of labour history*, vol. 6, London, 1982. I. Prothero, 'William Benbow and the concept of the "general strike"', *Past and Present*, vol. 63 (1974), is an invaluable study of Benbow's ideas.

16 Discussion of the first convention draws heavily on Epstein, *The lion of freedom*, pp. 138–75.

17 K. Judge, 'Early Chartist organization and the convention of 1839', *International Review of Social History*, vol. 20 (1975), and T. M. Kemnitz, 'The Chartist Convention of 1839', *Albion*, vol. 10 (1978), provide the best discussion of the convention's organisation and personnel.

18 T. M. Parssinen, 'Association, convention and anti-parliament in British radical politics, 1771–1848', *English Historical Review*, vol. 88 (July 1973), places the Chartist conventions in their radical context.

19 O'Connor's role in the convention is best approached through Epstein, *The lion of freedom*, pp. 138–93.

20 This was a short-lived event and Melbourne quickly returned to power. Peel was unwilling to form a minority Conservative administration.

21 Government policy is best approached through F. C. Mather, *Public order in the age of the Chartists*, Manchester, 1959, reprinted with minor corrections, Manchester, 1966.

22 Epstein, *The lion of freedom*, p. 196.

23 Thompson, *The Chartists*, p. 85.

24 William Dorling, *Henry Vincent: a biographical sketch*, London, 1879, remains the only detailed study of his life; Baylen and Grossman (eds.), *Biographical dictionary*, contains a short study.

25 David Williams, *John Frost: a study in Chartism*, Cardiff, 1939, reprinted New York, 1969, and David Williams, 'Chartism in Wales', in Asa Briggs (ed.), *Chartist studies*, 1959, pp. 220–48 provide the basis for the Newport Rising being a 'monster demonstration'. Ivor Wilks, *South Wales and the rising of 1839*, London, 1984, focuses on the nationalist dimension, while David J. V. Jones, *The last rising: the Newport insurrection of 1839*, Oxford, 1985, gives a detailed revisionist perspective.

26 J. E. Lloyd and R. T. Jenkins (eds.), *The dictionary of Welsh biography down to 1940*, Cardiff, 1959, features short biographies of the leading figures of the Newport Rising, including John Frost and Zephaniah Williams.

27 *Northern Star*, 3 May 1845.

28 On these abortive insurrections, Stephen Roberts, *Radical politicians and poets in early Victorian Britain*, Lampeter, 1993, provides an excellent study of Robert Peddie, a leading figure in the Bradford Rising.

29 A. J. Peacock, *Bradford Chartism, 1838–1840*, York, 1969, pp. 39–46.

5 Chartism: phase 2, 1840–42

The strident, revolutionary form of Chartism of 1839 and early 1840 had failed. The Chartists had assumed that the government would be unable to resist the sheer weight of numbers as in 1831 and 1832, that it would then move towards repressive policies, and that this repression would spark off an explosion of protest sufficient to engulf the forces of reaction. They were wrong. The government did not act as expected. Initially, the home secretary, Russell, used conciliatory tones, giving the more extreme Chartists time to alienate both middle-class reformers and those of moderate opinion by means of their militant rhetoric. The initiative quickly moved to the government and the Chartists found themselves on the defensive, caught between defeat and insurrection. By early 1840, it was clear that they could not defeat the state by force. Between 1840 and 1842, an intense, and often ill-tempered, debate took place between those who embraced mass action and those who favoured a more exclusive form of organisation. This was reflected in O'Connor's much publicised attack: 'Religious, Knowledge and Temperance Chartism HUMBUG: If Chartists you are, Chartists remain; you have work enough without entering into the new maze prepared for you . . . get your Charter, and I will answer for the religion, sobriety, knowledge and house, and a bit of land into the bargain.'[1] Had, as R. H. Tawney later suggested, 'the brains gone out of Chartism'?

'Knowledge Chartism': a move towards moderation

Chartism was a cultural, as well as a political, phenomenon. This emphasis reflected the diversity of the experiences and aspirations of the working class. The problem facing Chartism was how it should proceed. The first convention had been an organisational shambles without effective accountability or financial stability. O'Connor recognised the need for a permanent and centralised structure, with a national executive, weekly membership fees and elected officers, yet he needed to preserve the broadly democratic and inclusive character of the mass platform. It was also necessary to take account of the reality of working-class life, particularly the limited amount that workers could, or would, contribute to the movement when in employment. The National Charter Association, which had been set up while O'Connor was in prison, sought to resolve these contradictions and did so with some degree of success. It had a broad appeal to many within the working class, and O'Connor himself strongly approved of the principle of collective self-help within the democratic framework of the organisation. For others in the movement, the reassertion of the mass platform was increasingly unacceptable. It had failed in 1839 and 1840 and they believed that new approaches were necessary if the aims of the Charter were to be achieved. Divisions began to emerge between O'Connor, with his insistence on democracy, and the 'new movers', who denounced him and sought to restructure the Chartist reform alliance.

The 'new movers' wanted to revitalise the elite politics and ideological focus of the LWMA. They reflected the deep divisions within the working class, especially between skilled artisans and other industrial workers. The nature of politics changed as the older forms and rituals of open elections and the mass platform were challenged by more disciplined and organised forms of political expression: what D. A. Hamer called the 'politics of electoral pressure'.[2] In addition, public order was now more effectively policed and radical access to public space was being increasingly restricted. The development of 'respectability' within the movement provided an alternative, and more realistic, means of achieving the Charter's aims than the demagogic and increasingly arcane approach of O'Connor. The 'new movers' believed that winning the franchise was not simply a question of political rights, but also a test of character. The result was the emergence of new initiatives aimed at developing the 'character' necessary for the working class to be given the vote. It is hardly surprising that O'Connor was opposed to these initiatives, for they threatened the unity of Chartism.

William Lovett spent an unpleasant year in Warwick prison between August 1839 and July 1840.[3] His intense dislike of O'Connor, and his disillusionment with political agitation, also help to explain his changing attitudes. In the spring of 1840, he and John Collins wrote *Chartism: a new organisation of the people*, which made a powerful case for educational and moral reform and was published soon after their release.[4] At his trial, Lovett had stressed his belief in legal and non-violent methods of protest, and *Chartism* further underlined his shift towards a more exclusive 'moral-force' position. From 1840, Lovett saw educational reform as a necessary sequel to political change, and therefore became a sponsor of moderate tactics. He advocated an alternative culture that was grounded in elite, artisanal attitudes and also on the ethos of self-help. He did not stop being a vigorous spokesperson for the poor, but he did so in ways that were sufficiently moderate to make his views acceptable to the middle-class reformers. Lovett's focus on liberal individualism and class collaboration, rather than collectivism and the mass platform, caused him to become an increasingly marginalised, although not as David Goodway[5] suggests, an insignificant, figure in Chartist politics. Lovett and Collins argued that little had been achieved by 1840 because of working-class ignorance. What was needed was a grand scheme for moral and social reformation: self-supporting schools should be established and adult education – a particular interest of Lovett's – would prevent the development of 'vicious and intoxicating habits' and would result in self-improvement. A national association for 'promoting the political and social improvement of the people' was proposed as the means for putting these ideas into practice.

If it is useful to interpret Chartism after 1840 in the light of the distinction between physical and moral force, the adherents of the NCA were closer to the former position. James Epstein makes it very clear, however, that O'Connor had rational political objectives.[6] He, like Lovett, wanted to lead a unified working-class movement, and both men endorsed the interests of the working class through their own organisations. But their tactics diverged: for O'Connor, the aims of the Charter could only be won through the mass platform; for Lovett, success depended on the will of working men who were committed to personal improvement as well as to collective reform. It is therefore not surprising that O'Connor regarded Lovett's arguments, as expressed in *Chartism*, as a threat to the unity of the movement. This situation was made worse by Lovett's refusal to join the NCA. The antagonism between the two men was now irreconcilable.

In March 1841, Lovett and 73 other reformers published their 'Address to the Political and Social Reformers',[7] and the break became final. The 'Address' put the case for the National Association Promoting the Political and Social Improvement of the People in confident terms. O'Connor struck back immediately, labelling Lovett and his supporters 'Knowledge Chartists'. Lovett could not win against O'Connor in terms of numbers: membership of the national association, which was launched in the autumn of 1841 and which remained in existence until 1849, was never more than 500 (mostly artisans, their wives and children) and was dwarfed by that of the NCA. The struggle between Lovett and his supporters, on the one hand, and O'Connor, on the other, was an unequal one. Yet despite the NCA's numerical superiority, the danger for O'Connor was the increased possibility of co-operation between the national association and the middle classes. He was not opposed to an alliance with the lower-middle classes in principle, but only if he controlled the political agenda; what concerned O'Connor most was his deep-seated fear that Lovett's actions would shatter the unity of the working class.

'Church Chartism': a crucial Christian dimension

There was a vital and fundamental link between politics and religion during the nineteenth century. Chartism reflected this in its use of religious language and religious leaders. Indeed, Protestant evangelicalism was at its height during this period, and many 'Christian Chartists' gathered strength from their belief that they were truly the agents of God's work. In part, especially in 1838 and 1839, the battle lines were drawn on religious grounds. In some areas, clerical attitudes to working-class action appear to have been crucial. At least 40 clergymen sympathised actively with the Chartist movement, from the Unitarian minister, Henry Solly of Yeovil, and the Baptist Thomas Davies of Merthyr Tydfil, to the eloquent Congregationalist, Alexander Duncanson. They stood on the 'moral' wing of the movement, but that did not stop their chapel invective from being fiery. Joseph Rayner Stephens, a minister as well as a leading Chartist, for example, gave an apocalyptic sermon on 3 August 1839 before his trial at Chester: he warned of God's impending ruin of unrighteous civilisations and proclaimed the second coming. Some, like many preachers in the West Riding, shared the lives of their congregations: Benjamin Rushton, for instance, was a handloom-weaver, William Thornton a wool-comber and John Arran variously a blacksmith, teacher and a dealer in coffee and tea. Clerical support was strongest from the oldest and newest branches of nonconformity and this support raised hopes of an alliance between Chartism and nonconformists over issues like education, the relationship between the church and state, and political reform. This religious sentiment, as expressed by George Binns – the dominant Chartist figure on the Durham coalfields – at his open-air meetings with banners proclaiming 'We are born again', and 'Who is on the Lord's side?', runs through the Chartist movement. Binns' speeches described the need for regeneration, the unchristian nature of their opponents and the final triumph of the numbers and energy of the people: 'they may boast of their Wellingtons, but we have a God'. O'Connor may have distrusted 'Christian Chartists', but William Hill, the editor of his newspaper, the *Northern Star*, defended them vigorously.

It would be a mistake to underestimate the importance of religious radicalism: even the NCA's membership card carried the words 'This is Our Charter, God is Our Guide.' It was also evident in the frequent inclusion of some form of religious ceremony in Chartist rituals, from blessing the food at radical dinners, and singing 'Chartist hymns', to holding Chartist funerals. The NCA executive did not speak for all Chartists when it refused to agree to the creation of 'Christian Chartist' churches at the expense of political organisations.[8] Parish-church demonstrations took place in at least 31 localities during the second half of 1839. The 'corrupted' church was contrasted with the 'true' church that was the property of the people; tithes and compulsory church rates, the roles of Anglican clergymen as magistrates, pew rents and the limited membership of the parish vestry – all contributed to this assault.

The attack on the established church must be seen in the context of the structure of Tory–Anglican power, which had opposed reform in 1832 and now opposed the Charter. The Anglican church and orthodox Methodist churches led the attack on the atheism ('infidelism') and violence of working-class radicals. Jabez Bunting, leader of the Wesleyan Methodists, had no qualms in expelling lay preachers or ministers who sympathised with, or actively supported, the Chartists and when the minister Joseph Barker was expelled from the Methodist New Connection in 1841, he took 29 churches with him, many of which became Chartist in spirit, if not in name. In Cornwall and Denbighshire, in Wales, preachers went further in demonstrating their hostility to the Chartists, disrupting political meetings and visiting houses to warn people against signing national petitions.

'Christian Chartism' in Scotland

The men who established Chartism in Scotland in the late 1830s were almost all closely connected to various churches.[9] Indeed, the newspaper *Chartist Circular* advised people to 'Study the New Testament. It contains the elements of Chartism'. In the early stages of the movement, Scottish Chartists looked to the churches for support and leadership and Chartist committees quickly appointed deputations to meet the ministers of their parishes in order to seek their support. No co-operation was expected from the clergymen of the established church, but the response of the dissenting clergy was a profound disappointment: this was, in general, apathetic, a combination of diffidence in committing themselves to the Chartist cause and an innate prejudice against Christians 'meddling in politics'. The important part played in Chartism by the Reverend Patrick Brewer of Paisley Abbey and the Reverend Archibald Browning of Tillicountry was the exception. James Moir, one of the most radical Glaswegian reformers, had warned his fellow clergymen in April 1839 that their failure to support the People's Charter could lead to the development of a new religious denomination that combined the principles of Christianity and Chartism. The following month, first in Hamilton and then in Paisley, Chartists began conducting their own religious services; the practice spread quickly, and by early 1840 'Christian Chartist' congregations had occurred in at least 30 places. Arthur O'Neill,[10] the youngest member of the Universal Suffrage Central Committee for Scotland (a body established in 1839 to co-ordinate Chartist activities throughout Scotland), a former student of theology and an inspiring lay preacher, reported in late 1839: 'Chartist congregations to become general in every corner of the land [needed] only Chartist preachers – men who would tell the truth, and the whole truth, and who would not scruple to raise their voices against any voice, whether in Church or State.'[11] The intention was not to develop an alternative to the older forms of organised religion, but to put pressure on hostile or diffident clergymen. This strategy proved very successful and some clergymen – even the most hostile – began to adopt a more sympathetic, or at least neutral, attitude towards Chartism.

By March 1840, permanent congregations had been established in some places, and these formed the beginnings of the 'Christian Chartist' churches. Some Chartists thought that a Chartist synod should be set up to embrace all the local Chartist churches, and in January 1841 a delegate conference of all the Chartist churches in Scotland was held to consider how they could help each other and whether any central organisation was necessary; it reached no real conclusions. No further such conferences were held, however, and after 1841 there appears to have been a steady decline in the number of localities in which Chartist services were held. Despite this apparent lessening of support, when Reverend William Hill, the editor of the *Northern Star*, toured Scotland in August 1842, he found that the 'Christian Chartist' churches remained the main strength of Scottish Chartism.

'Church Chartism' in England

The focus of 'Church Chartism' had already moved south into England by the early 1840s. O'Neill, for example, preached to Chartist congregations on Sundays and built up the organisation during the week. He was appointed a delegate to the demonstration that had been arranged for the release of John Collins and William Lovett from Warwick jail in July 1840 and his sincerity made a great impression on the Birmingham Chartists. Although he went back to Scotland for a short time, he returned to Birmingham (at Collins' invitation) in late 1840 to give a series of lectures and sermons to mark the opening of the Birmingham Chartist Church on 27 December 1840 at Newhall Street, where he had been appointed pastor. He believed that the 'true' church could not remain apart from daily events but 'must enter into the struggles of the people and guide them'; unsurprisingly, the Chartist church was overtly political, its ideology and practice reflecting the strengths and weakness of the Birmingham radical movement. Although O'Neill believed in the importance of maintaining links with the middle class, his attitude towards it was not, however, uncritical: in the tract *The question: what good will the Charter do?,* he challenged the new industrial society, criticising the middle class for its failure to fulfil the promises of the 1832 Reform Act and denouncing the inhumanity of both the new Poor Law and the factory system. Despite this attack, O'Neill always leaned – even in his most radical phases – towards an alliance with the middle class.

For his part, O'Connor saw the Chartist church as a diversion from the 'true' aims of the movement. He opposed the Birmingham church on particular, as well as on general, grounds, arguing that it was objectionable to set up a church that barred Irish Catholics; his outlook was supported by George White, the leader of the NCA in Birmingham. O'Neill returned their antipathy by not allowing members of the Chartist church to join the NCA. There were occasions upon which the two groups came together, however: the joint petitioning for the release of Frost, Williams and Jones, for example, and their common opposition to the Anti-Corn Law League. Yet the basic opposition of the church to physical force and O'Neill's support for a middle-class alliance remained a serious obstacle to closer ties. Despite these differences, O'Neill remained a Chartist and sided with the Chartist majority when Joseph Sturge and many of the middle-class members of the Complete Suffrage Union withdrew from the December 1842 conference after the vote to endorse the Charter, although the experience confirmed his fears about the Chartist leadership.

His rift with Sturge was short-lived, however, and in January 1843 O'Neill attended a meeting of the council of the Complete Suffrage Union, where his plans for strengthening its organisation were accepted. He was sentenced to a year's imprisonment for using seditious language in August 1843 and on his release returned to the Newhall Street church, declaring that he was 'still a Chartist'. The context of Birmingham Chartism had, however, changed and no longer promised implicit support for the national movement led by O'Connor. The Chartists' revival of 'harmonious co-operation' between the classes was renewed and absorbed both the Complete Suffrage Union and the Chartist church, which were dissolved in December 1845 and the following year respectively. This change in O'Neill's attitude can be seen in 1848 when, as elsewhere, Chartism was revived in Birmingham; along with other former Christian Chartists, O'Neill joined middle-class radicals in forming the short-lived Reform League which supported the MP Joseph Hume's agitation for the limited household suffrage advocated in the 'Little Charter'.

Was 'Church Chartism' a threat to the unity of the Chartist movement? It may have been strong in Scotland, but its effect was more limited in England, although the success of O'Neill in Birmingham was paralleled by that of James Scholefield in Manchester and Benjamin Rushton in Halifax. Among the weaving communities, Chartism often took the form of a 'holy war', complete with all the trappings of revivalism; R. F. Wearmouth has identified over 500 camp meetings during the early years of Chartism and in the late 1840s.[12] For 'Christian Chartists', politics was not simply about power but was also about moral regeneration. O'Connor could not stomach this.

'Teetotal Chartism': reforming through abstinence

Temperance and teetotalism campaigners offered another way of changing society.[13] The temperance movement had its origins in the late 1820s and sought to reduce spending (especially on the part of the working classes) on alcoholic drink; it tried to get people to take 'the pledge' to give up drink altogether, or to abstain from drinking spirits. Imposing abstinence from alcohol had long been an integral part of the radical ethos; indeed, John Fraser (1818–85), the bishop of Manchester who spent much of his life campaigning for temperance, went as far as to suggest that 'Drinking radicalism is a contradiction in terms'. It is therefore not surprising that a temperance strand should have developed within Chartism, or that this should have been a cause of division in the movement. Radicals had been arguing about temperance as early as 1831, while drink and the sellers of drink were so central to the working-class culture that conflict was almost inevitable.

The growth in popularity of the temperance and total-abstinence movements during the 1830s and 1840s encouraged some radicals to consider a 'general union' between temperance and political reformers. The National Charter Association argued for sobriety, but consistently opposed calls to make total abstinence part of the Chartist programme. This policy made very good sense, for working men were divided on the temperance question. Some saw drink as an integral part of working-class life. A Trowbridge Chartist, for example, promised his audience 'plenty of roast beef, plum pudding and strong beer for working three hours a day', while public houses had furthermore long formed the focal point for radical activities. Ernest Jones, too, repeatedly emphasised that 'the Charter was not to be found at the bottom of a glass of water'. Many Chartist leaders also disliked the temperance movement's religious connections: certainly, for many middle-class nonconformists, temperance was a religious and moral question that was completely divorced from politics, and in 1839, the Chartist delegates Robert Lowery and Abram Duncan were opposed by the leaders of teetotalism in Cornwall. Negative Chartist attitudes to the temperance movement on religious grounds merged into their objections to it on the grounds of class: teetotallers were accused of narrow-mindedness and middle-class pretensions, and there was a real fear that that working-class aspiration would be subordinated to the teetotal movement's middle-class leaders. It was precisely such a dilution of the Chartist movement that O'Connor feared.

Brian Harrison argues that 'Teetotal Chartism' was 'never a negligible force' and that it 'made no sharp break with previous radical attitudes'.[14] Sobriety made sound political sense: it appealed to public opinion – especially among the middle classes – and weakened government arguments about the irresponsibility of the working class. In early 1840, John Fraser described seeing 'pot-house [pub] politicians hiccupping for liberty' as 'a revolting spectacle'.[15] For his part, William Lovett, in *Chartism*, suggested the creation of drink-free district halls to encourage self-improvement and alcohol-free entertainment. Many individuals campaigned for both temperance and the Charter and, in the early months of 1841, when enthusiasm for both movements was at its height, 'Teetotal Chartist' societies sprang up in London, the north, the Midlands and Scotland. The leading figure in the creation of such societies was Henry Vincent,[16] who had been an abstainer since 1836 and who had long argued for working-class self-improvement and sobriety. Prison heightened his temperance and, in December 1840, together with C. H. Neesom, Cleave, Hill and Hetherington, he signed an address which argued that the aristocracy only ruled because of the vices of the poor, and that Chartists must therefore become teetotallers. Vincent's manifesto reflected the growing divisions within Chartism and the corresponding search for an alternative social and political programme to the fundamentalism promoted by O'Connor.

What was the appeal of 'Teetotal Chartism'? Many contemporary commentators, from the working, as well as middle, class, were concerned with the causes of poverty; the evils associated with drunkenness were obvious, and this led many reformers to exaggerate alcohol's significance as a cause of poverty. There was also a widespread belief that drunkenness helped to explain the weakness of the Chartist movement in 1839 and 1840. Temperance was furthermore regarded as an expression of the dignity of class. Teetotalism, its supporters believed, also posed a direct assault on the ability of the government to govern: at least a third of government revenue came from drink taxes; without this, some Chartists argued, the government would not be able to pay its police or soldiers. Teetotalism was thus a powerful means of redefining the radical alliance between the working and middle classes.

'Teetotal Chartism' developed quickly during the spring of 1841. His teetotal tour during March and April took Vincent through Oxford, Banbury, Leicester, Nottingham, Cheltenham and Gloucester. O'Connor's attack on 'Teetotal Chartism', made in March and early April, was a stinging one, prompted by his belief that teetotalism was divisive and a reflection of the influence of the London radicals whom he so despised. Vincent's influence on the movement soon declined, however – in late April he became a lecturer for the Complete Suffrage Union – and the movement collapsed almost overnight. This apparently rapid disintegration is, in some respects, deceiving, for in certain areas teetotalism remained a powerful adjunct to Chartism.

The rift between Vincent and O'Connor has been seen as a division between a moderate who blundered into a temperance backwater on the one hand, and a class-conscious repudiator of evangelistic crusading on the other. Such an interpretation, Harrison suggests, is wrong on three counts. Firstly, 'Teetotal Chartism' only seemed moderate: Lovett and Vincent were consistently anti-aristocratic and were aware of the dignity of their class. Secondly, both Lovett's autobiography and Mark Hovell's influential narrative give the impression that O'Connor was opposed to temperance. This was far from the case: O'Connor did not oppose teetotalism as a principle, but in order to avoid embroiling Chartism with the cause of temperance.[17] This was a shrewd political judgement, and there is ample evidence of the disunity that 'Teetotal Chartism' caused at both national and local levels to justify his concern. Thirdly, the Lovett–Hovell interpretation ignores O'Connor's later attitudes. His temperance views certainly influenced his practice in the Land Plan, when he barred distillers, brewers and drink-sellers from his estates and, in 1847, urged settlers on the Herongate estate (the first of the sites established under the Land Plan) to avoid the adjacent beershop. Temperance, he believed, was only possible when working people were no longer exploited. In 1846 he said: 'Ah! If I was monarch for twenty-four hours, I'd level every gin palace with the dust . . . and in less than a month I'd produce a wise representation of a sober and thoughtful national mind.'[18] Tactics, not principle, determined O'Connor's attitude to 'Teetotal Chartism' in 1841.

Other forms of Chartism

O'Connor reserved his venom for 'Knowledge', 'Church' and 'Teetotal' Chartists. In part, his opposition was dictated by his principles: these movements stood for a different brand of Chartism – elitist, artisanal and exclusive. O'Connor declared that there might even be 'washing and cleansing Chartists declaring that you were too dirty for enfranchisement'.[19] It was also a question of personality and temperament. Above all, however, his hostility to these potentially divided groups was prompted by his belief in the necessity of forming a united front against the common enemy: those with the vote. O'Connor recognised that it was unlikely that Chartism could have survived the revival of LWMA-style elitism, which might have achieved more for working people in the long run, but which could never have held a mass movement together, nor could it have rivalled O'Connor's championing of the 'fustian coats' (the working class). However, even in areas where O'Connor had significant support, local Chartists turned to other strategies in an attempt to achieve their objectives. These may have not have been as divisive as the elitism of Lovett and Vincent, but they reflected the growing diversity of the movement.

In some provincial cities, for example, Chartists turned to municipal politics[20] in reflection of the growing recognition that parliament would have to be persuaded rather than abused. The popularity of the principal Chartist weapons – marches and petitions, conventions, delegations and public meetings – were evidence of the irresistible support for the Chartist cause, and the less raucous variants of such demonstrations were intended to convince the 'ins' (the franchised) that the 'outs' should be given the vote because they displayed moral responsibility. Taking part in local politics could also show this. Chartists were most active in the municipal politics of the towns, where the urban political structure allowed them scope to infiltrate various local institutions.

The Chartist involvement in Leeds' municipal politics

It was in Leeds especially that real efforts were made to make the Charter work within a local context.[21] Chartist efforts in the election for improvement commissioners[22] in January 1840 were frustrated by an adverse legal decision that barred Chartists who were elected from holding office. During the following years, they shared power with liberals, but in 1842 gained full control of the improvement commission. The debate over the Leeds Improvement Bill (that aimed to deal with sanitary problems) in 1841 and 1842 raised important constitutional questions about where real municipal power lay. The Leeds Chartist improvement commissioners amended the bill to democratise local government, as follows:

- Powers were to be given to the improvement commission, but not to the council or magistrates.
- Rate-payers were to elect improvement commissioners who would have to satisfy a residential, but not a financial, qualification.
- No municipal expenditure over £500 would be possible without the direct consent of the rate-payers, and meetings to seek their consent would be held in the evening rather than during the working day.
- Finally, rates were to be levied progressively, with houses rated at under £10 being assessed at one-third the rate for houses over £50.

The council and the magistrates opposed the bill, however, while property owners were lukewarm in their support and the legal representatives of the commissioners withdrew their services. Without political, financial and legal support the bill had to be retracted, but the Chartists were able to persuade the vestry (the parish council, a body of considerable importance in nineteenth-century municipal politics) to resolve that no local bill would be acceptable that did not contain agreed democratic arrangements. Despite this agreement, the bill was revived with its democratic clauses removed, whereupon it was approved by parliament. The Leeds Improvement Act of 1842 vested all power in the town council, with which the improvement commission was merged.

The Chartists subsequently turned their attention to other areas of urban government in Leeds. In 1842 they secured the office of churchwarden and held it for five years until defeated by the Tories in 1847. They also moved onto the board of surveyors of highways, and from 1843 until well after the national demise of Chartism, Chartist surveyors were elected. When a board of guardians was set up in late 1844, it was characteristic that Chartists stood for election to it: three did so in 1844 and 1845, and in the 1846 election ten stood, although only one was elected. In Leeds during the 1840s, Chartists were thus commissioners, churchwardens, surveyors and guardians, offices that gave Chartists considerable power in local government. This was fulfilling a Chartist vision of participation by 'the people', and if poor men could run local government why should they not be given the right to vote? The Leeds Chartists were not necessarily poor men, however: in order to stand for municipal office they had to live in properties rated at £30 or £40.

From 1842 it was the council that held the real power in Leeds and, for a decade, Chartists – either individually, or as a body – took part in municipal elections. But the Chartists were not united, and did not vote as a bloc, especially when it came to issues involving expenditure. John Jackson, a leading local Chartist, for example, voted against imposing a rate for drainage and a new sewerage system in 1844, but in favour of a larger courthouse and altering the market between 1845 and 1846. George Robson, another Chartist, voted against Jackson on the former issue, but supported the latter, while William Brook – also a Chartist – voted against Jackson on both issues. The Chartists were furthermore split on each of the six votes held between January 1851 and May 1852 on the building of the town hall. It was, however, Chartists who proposed some of the most important municipal innovations: Joshua Hobson, for instance, pressed for the creation of a shopping street in 1845, to include a new town hall; he, along with Robson and Brook, also argued for an effective drainage system. It was the Chartist guardian, John Ayrey, who first suggested the building of an industrial school, the only major Poor Law building project in the West Riding during the 1840s.

What gave consistency to the otherwise diverse beliefs of the Leeds Chartists was their advocation of democratic control. Brook favoured municipal spending when the economy was prosperous, for example, but opposed it between 1848 and 1849 when the economy slumped and he did not want to increase his constituents' rates. The advocation of popular involvement and control can be seen in many of the other ideas expressed by municipal Chartists: there were attempts to ensure popular participation in the 1842 Leeds Improvement Bill; in education, they favoured locally elected boards and rate-aided schools 30 years before the 1870 Elementary Education Act; they were strongly opposed to centralisation and in favour of locally controlled towns. The experience of Leeds was paralleled in other major towns: in Birmingham, Leicester, Manchester, Salford and Nottingham, and especially in Sheffield, Chartists became embroiled in municipal politics.

The National Charter Association: a working-class party?

Despite the Chartists' diversity, a significant degree of unity and national organisation was provided by the National Charter Association, which was formed in July 1840 largely at O'Connor's instigation. At local and district levels the process of its establishment began in the spring of 1840. There is no doubting the vitality of the enthusiasm of the NCA, although, as Mark Hovell noted, it 'was much more localised than in 1839 but within its narrow bounds it was stronger and healthier'.[23] This provided the impetus for national reorganisation and during the late spring and summer the Chartist press was filled with calls and plans for a national body. O'Connor – now in prison – monitored developments closely and supported moves for a national Chartist conference to be held in Manchester in July. The problem, as O'Connor rightly recognised, was how a permanent organisation should be funded. Various schemes were discussed when the conference delegates met on 20 July and the agreement that was subsequently established signified the desire of the movement's leadership, as well as of its grass-roots membership, to move towards a permanent and centralised organisation.

- An NCA executive council, consisting of seven full-time, paid members, would be responsible for the co-ordination of the national Chartist movement. It was to be elected annually by means of a ballot of all NCA members, with each county being able to nominate one candidate.
- Members of the NCA had to sign a declaration agreeing to the association's principles and buy a 2d (pence) quarterly membership card.
- Where possible, members were to be organised locally into classes of 10 under a class leader who was responsible for collecting each member's 1d subscription. Classes were to be grouped into wards or divisions, and monthly ward meetings would hear reports from class leaders.
- There was to be a 'collector' for each ward, who would be responsible for forwarding subscriptions to the national executive.
- Each large town, county or riding was to have its own council, whose officers would be elected democratically.

Although the success in establishing the local organisations was variable, this pioneering structure took democratic, mass-party organisation into new areas of political life. It sought to address the problems posed by funding political organisations and recognised the need to accommodate local and occupational diversity within a national framework.[24]

The NCA remained the major national Chartist organisation for the remainder of the decade (although its membership and influence declined after 1842), and some historians have seen it as the first independent working-class political party. The NCA was not, however, unique: working-class voluntary organisations had become increasingly sophisticated, and the NCA drew from their experience. The Methodists, for example, had been using class organisation within a national framework both for evangelistic work and for collecting subscriptions for half a century. The Owenite movement, which was reorganised from 1835, also operated a system of districts, paid national officials and subscriptions. Attempts to form national trade unions, especially by the Miners' Association in 1842, had organisational parallels with the NCA. The major difference between these bodies and the NCA was that they tended to be exclusive organisations while the NCA sought inclusiveness.

The NCA gradually grew during 1840. By the end of the year, just under 70 local associations had become affiliated with it. These were concentrated in Lancashire, Yorkshire, the Nottinghamshire–Derby area and London. Birmingham, the West Midlands and Scotland showed little interest, however.

County and district organisations were established in Lancashire, the West Riding, the East Midlands, Durham and Gloucester, and full-time NCA 'missionaries' were employed in each of these areas apart from Gloucester. Some Chartists, however, were hesitant about joining with the NCA for three main reasons:

- opposition to the principle of centralisation and the loss of local independence and control;
- objections to the appointment of paid itinerant orators, or men 'making a trade of politics';
- the question of the legality of NCA activities, especially regarding correspondence between NCA secretaries [25] (late eighteenth-century legislation had made correspondence between radical societies illegal).

The latter problem was addressed at a delegate meeting held in late February 1841 that adopted a new plan of organisation. The major change was to stress that all NCA members belonged to one society which, it was hoped, would get round the law, since all correspondence would be within one national organisation rather than between affiliated branches and localities. This solution appears to have calmed many Chartists' fears, and from February 1841 to the end of the year the number of associations affiliated to the NCA grew from 8 to nearly 300, with 20,000 members. By June 1842, there were over 400 local associations and 50,000 members, and by the autumn of 1842, when the NCA reached its peak in terms of numbers, some 70,000 membership cards had been issued. The defeat of the mass strikes of 1842, concerns surrounding the NCA's accounts that prompted a fierce debate in the columns of the *Northern Star*, attacks on the leadership in 1842 and 1843, as well as the general decrease in radical activity, seriously affected its further growth and the NCA's influence declined. Reorganised in 1843, it moved its base to London.

The NCA was very much O'Connor's organisation, and was often denounced as 'O'Connor's party'. It was established as a model of democratic leadership and O'Connor defended it vigorously, a stance which led to significant personal opposition. Many Chartists, including Lovett, refused to join, causing O'Connor to fear that the movement would fragment. Lovett's association (the National Association Promoting the Political and Social Improvement of the People) had considerable middle-class backing, while the success of the Chartist municipal candidates in Leeds owed something to the efforts being made to reforge a Chartist–radical alliance. Although O'Connor took the view that the Anti-Corn Law League offered working people only minimum support in order to achieve its own ends, the winter of 1841 to 1842 also saw agreement being reached in several cities between Chartists and Corn Law repealers. Yet O'Connor's relationship with the NCA was highly ambiguous: he was not a member of the executive council until September 1843, for example. Indeed, his status, and the legitimacy of his leadership, came from being an independent gentleman very much in the tradition of Hunt and Cobbett. This older tradition of the 'platform' co-existed with the newer, and more formally organised, forms of radical protest that were characterised by the NCA. O'Connor's role in this process of transition was pivotal.

Was O'Connor right?

O'Connor faced major problems after he was released from prison.

- The dispiriting events of 1839 and early 1840 had deprived Chartism of its sense of urgency. The proliferation of 'Chartisms' in 1840 and 1841 reflected the inherent diversity of the working class, and there remained an almost unbridgeable gulf between skilled workers and the rest.
- Radical activity had always been diffuse, and the recognition that universal suffrage was not imminent led many radicals to drift into other forms of social protest and self-help activity.

The unity of Chartism was being sorely tested.

Historians have often seen the growing fragmentation of the movement in a negative light; they are, to a degree, right. O'Connor's style of leadership, which was often – but unjustifiably – criticised as being undemocratic and 'dictatorial', was a major area of contention. His attempt to maintain a sense of working-class unity at all costs was bound to rankle with other Chartist leaders and with the local associations, which cherished their independence. Bronterre O'Brien argued that 'Chartism has been wrecked – frittered away – all but annihilated by the attempt to force the whole Chartist body into one association'.[26] It is, however, better to regard the events of 1840 and 1841 more positively, as a broadening of the cultural dimensions of Chartism. 'Knowledge', 'Church' and 'Teetotal' Chartism – particularly at the local level – can be seen not as diversions from, but as complementary to, the movement's more overt challenge in terms of national mass action. O'Connor's attack in the spring of 1841 was not on education, religion or temperance, but on those who used these issues to develop exclusive forms of working-class activity. The division between 'moral-force' and 'physical-force' Chartists – however neat it may have appeared to later historians – does not do justice to the complementary and complex nature of radical activities. Many of those who argued for co-operation, religion, education and temperance between 1840 and 1841 were involved in mass class confrontation in 1842 and 1848. Circumstances, rather than principles, determined whether the 'cultural' or 'confrontational' dimensions of Chartism were to the fore.

O'Connor's position as the pre-eminent Chartist leader was confirmed by the events of 1840 and 1841. There were, however, limits to his ascendancy over the movement. Many Chartists may have deferred to O'Connor, but there was also a turbulent spirit of democracy in Chartist protests that he could not afford to ignore. His leadership was thus subjected to close scrutiny and criticism by local Chartists who were keen to show that they were not his 'dupes'. Those who regard O'Connor's leadership as being dictatorial therefore neglect just how conditional it was.

Chartism and the middle classes, 1840–42

The differences between O'Connor and the relatively small section of the Chartist leadership that was involved in the 'new move' – Lovett, Vincent, Hetherington, Collins, O'Neill and Lowery – reflected their contrasts in style and emphasis. 'Rational' protest was becoming increasingly opposed to O'Connor's assurance that the mass platform was *the* means of achieving the Charter. Such alternative perspectives shared much common ground with middle-class radicalism, and this posed a greatly divisive threat to Chartism, especially between 1842 and 1843.

The broadening of the Chartism movement during the early 1840s left the central problem of how to achieve the aims of the Charter unanswered. What James Epstein calls 'the middle-class embrace' was one potential means of breaking the impasse. Between 1840 and 1850 there were various attempts by middle-class radicals to reforge the alliance with working-class radicalism: the Leeds Parliamentary Reform Association (LPRA), 1840–41; the Complete Suffrage Union (CSU), 1841–43; as well as the 'Little Charter' and the National Parliamentary Reform Association, 1848–50. The sticking point was O'Connor's inflexible insistence on retaining the full Charter and also his assertion that Chartism must maintain its independence from all forms of middle-class radicalism. He thus opposed advances from sections of the Anti-Corn Law League and from those who called for 'limited' suffrage. His views were clear by early 1840: 'Join them now, and they will laugh at you; stand out like men and THEY MUST JOIN YOU for the Charter.'[27]

The Leeds Parliamentary Reform Association

The failure to obtain the reform of the Corn Laws from the Whig government in 1840 led some middle-class radicals to regard suffrage reform as a better possibility for success. The Leeds Parliamentary Reform Association, which was formed in May 1840 and held its first public meeting in late August, was one such expression of this view.[28] The 'Leeds new move' favoured household suffrage, the ballot, equal constituencies, triennial elections and the abolition of the property qualification for the franchise. It reflected the opinion of certain sections of the Leeds middle class, however, and while it could count on the support of working men's association members, and also on those workers who followed middle-class radical leadership, it encountered widespread opposition. Edward Baines, the proprietor of the influential *Leeds Mercury* newspaper, and his son, for example, did not support the association, believing that free trade could be achieved without a dangerous tinkering with the 1832 reform settlement. Richard Cobden and the Lancashire leadership of the Anti-Corn Law League took a similar position. There was implacable opposition to the LPRA from the main Chartist leaders and from the columns of the *Northern Star*. As a result, the association petered out in early 1841 and was eventually absorbed by the Complete Suffrage Union.

The Complete Suffrage Union

Class co-operation had been the Birmingham message under Attwood, and now Joseph Sturge, the leader of the Complete Suffrage Union, was updating the Attwood agenda.[29] The CSU developed from anti-Corn Law agitation during the autumn of 1841.[30] Reverend Edward Miall, the editor of the *Nonconformist* paper, and Joseph Sturge, a wealthy Birmingham corn dealer, aimed at uniting the middle and working classes in a crusade to obtain a 'full, fair and free representation' of the people in parliament. Sturge wanted to reconcile the middle and working classes through the repeal of class-based legislation and a declaration that the exclusion of the bulk of the population from the franchise was both unconstitutional and unchristian. The movement reflected anxieties among parts of the middle class about the class tensions of the early 1840s and also their growing belief that the repeal of the Corn Laws would not occur without suffrage reform. What made the Complete Suffrage Union different from earlier attempts at class reconciliation was its acceptance of universal suffrage. This posed a real problem for O'Connor and throughout 1842, while expressing personal respect for Sturge, he consistently opposed any Chartist alliance with the CSU.

Some Chartists, largely those who already approved of class collaboration, were sympathetic to the CSU. Lovett and Francis Place lent their support to it, and at the first meeting organised by the CSU in Birmingham, the moderate nature of the movement was emphasised by the systematic exclusion of O'Connorites. By late April 1842, it had 50 local associations and the CSU presented a rival parliamentary petition to that of the NCA. O'Connor initially conducted a fierce campaign against the CSU, which was obliged to adopt the Charter in all but name, but then recognised the tactical advantage of reaching an accommodation with middle-class radicals and came out in favour of class collaboration in July 1842. He did not seek an alliance with the CSU, however, but rather the incorporation of a section of the middle class into the Chartist movement. By the autumn of 1842, under pressure from Chartist hard-liners and disappointed by his failure to attract substantial middle-class converts to Chartism, he reversed his position and again attacked the CSU as 'a League job' – that is, implying that it had an Anti-Corn Law League agenda.

At a CSU conference in December, which was packed with Chartist delegates, the middle-class radicals insisted on the adoption of a 'New Bill of Rights' for universal suffrage, instead of the emotive Charter. This was an attempt to disassociate middle-class radicalism from the anarchic confusion that was associated with O'Connor and his supporters. Lovett was not prepared to accept the change in terminology and joined with O'Connor in substituting 'charter' for 'bill', thus causing the immediate secession of the majority of the middle-class CSU delegates. Class collaboration was thereby ended and O'Connor's grip on the Chartist movement was tightened.

The Plug Plot, 1842

The experiment with class collaboration in 1842 took place in an atmosphere of widespread industrial unrest and heightened Chartist activity. Plans for the second National Petition and a CSU convention had been launched in the previous September. The latter eventually met in Birmingham in April 1842. It was much better organised, with the number of its delegates limited to 24 from the English constituencies and 25 from the Welsh and Scottish ones. The petition was also better organised and contained 3 million signatures. The result was, however, the same as before: rejection by the House of Commons by 287 to 46 votes on 1 May 1842. This created much bitterness in the Chartist localities, a situation that was made worse by the worst economic recession of the century.

In 1842, the challenge to local and national governmental authority arose directly from the opposition of the working-class districts of the north and the Midlands to unemployment, high food prices and wage reductions.[31] Up to 500,000 workers were involved in the series of strikes which swept across many of the industrial districts of the north and the Midlands in July and August 1842. North Staffordshire coal-miners struck in July, followed by Lancashire textile-industry workers, in response to wage cuts. Mobs of strikers travelled through the county enforcing a general stoppage by drawing out the plugs (hence the name the 'Plug Plot') of factory boilers, thus rendering them useless. Within weeks the strikes had spread across the Pennines into Yorkshire and north into Scotland. By September, 15 English and Welsh counties and 8 Scottish counties were affected.

What was the extent of Chartist involvement in the Plug Plot? There was little agreement on this either among contemporaries or subsequently among historians. It is clear that many of those who spoke at an NCA meeting held in Manchester in August 1842 were Chartists who had little or no connection with the textile trades. In Lancashire, however, it was local Chartist leaders such as Richard Pilling and William Aitken (who worked in the textile trade and had long been associated with the Ten Hour movement) who linked the call for fair wages to demands for a general strike to achieve the aims of the Charter. Nationally, Chartist leaders were caught unawares by the strikes but soon exploited the situation for their own ends. O'Connor himself supported extending the strikes but deplored the use of violent language and the strikers' belief that they were the forerunners of revolution. A series of regional trade conferences held in August presented an opportunity for Chartist intervention, and there was a widespread adoption of the Charter as one of the strike's main aims. Although there was some convergence of Chartist and trade-union activity in Manchester, Glasgow and London, the extent to which Chartists were involved in the Plug Plot varied regionally. In Yorkshire, for example, where trade unions were weaker and less widespread than in Lancashire, local Chartists exercised strong influence over the strikers' tactics, but generally the Chartist leaders were too divided among themselves to take full advantage of the strike movement. The unions themselves had little central organisational machinery capable of co-ordinating the strikes, and the different attitudes of the Chartists prevented the NCA from taking on this role. Chartists were thus reacting to the situation, not determining it.

The tension eased in September; the 1842 harvest had been good, trade was already reviving, and employers agreed to cancel wage reductions. However, the strike movement had two negative results for the Chartists. Firstly, the effort made by some Chartists to exploit the strikes for their own ends allowed the Conservative prime minister, Peel (whose party had won the 1841 general election), and his home secretary, Sir James Graham, to blame them for the unrest. There was a wave of arrests in September and harsh sentences were handed out: in Staffordshire, for example, of 274 cases tried, 154 men were imprisoned and 5 men were transported for life. By early 1843, however, there was less need for such harsh treatment as the strikes were over and the unrest had quietened. Peel and Graham recognised, as had Russell from 1839 to 1840, that pushing repression too far was counterproductive, since it alienated public opinion from the government and created public sympathy for the protesters. Secondly, trade-union disillusionment with Chartism probably increased. For unionists, the issue was economic rather than political and, for them, the strikes were not entirely unsuccessful.

Confrontational tactics had failed between 1839 and 1840 and also in 1842. Mass arrests and imprisonment sapped the strength of the Chartist movement, and the relative economic prosperity of the years between 1842 and 1848 helped to dampen the enthusiasm of the rank and file. Furthermore, the agreement between Lovett and O'Connor in late 1842 over the CSU's proposals was short-lived: Lovett had no intention of working with O'Connor, and gradually he and other like-minded individuals withdrew to pursue their objectives by means of non-confrontational agitation. O'Connor now emerged firmly in control of the formal Chartist movement, which he promptly led in entirely new directions.

Document case study
The 'Plug Plot' strike movement, 1842: contrasting perspectives

5.1 A middle-class perspective

We have to record the disastrous occurrence of a turn-out of manufacturing labourers in and about Manchester, which must be regarded with sorrow by wise and thoughtful men. It would appear that the sudden and turbulent display of congregated thousands, leaving their daily employment – marching upon mills, forcing willing and unwilling alike to join them, and, in a moment, paralysing the whole activity of the natural enterprise of their neighbourhood arose, in the first instance from a reduction of wages in one quarter, given almost without notice . . . We are no partisans; we do not oppose, abstractly for their peculiar doctrines, either the chartist or the anti-corn-law leaguer; we leave all political opinion, however violent, its fair play; but we despise the infamous diplomacy that would make its game out of the miseries of the people. Nothing can more excite our indignant rebuke than the revolutionary villain or the quack preacher of politics who says: 'I have a charter to achieve here, or a corn-law to repeal there, and, now that the people are starving and in tatters, I will convert their rags into banners of rebellion and their hunger into the sign of blood'. Yet this, we believe, is the course that was pursued, furnishing the key to all the riots and seditions that disturbed the land.

Source: *Illustrated London News*, August 1842, printed in a fuller version in Richard Brown and Christopher Daniels, *The Chartists*, London, 1984, pp. 79–80

5.2 Thomas Cooper: a view from Leicester

The decrease of work, and the absolute destitution of an immense number of the working classes in Leicester, led to alarming symptoms, in the summer of 1842. The Union Poor House, or 'Bastile' [*sic*], as it was always called by the working men, was crowded to excess and the throngs who asked for outdoor relief for a time seemed to paralyse the authorities. A mill was at length set up at the workhouse, and it had to be turned by the applicants for relief. The working of the wheel they declared to be beyond their strength; and no doubt some of the poor feeble stockingers among them spoke the truth. They complained of it also as degrading; and it kindled a spirit of strong indignation among the great body of working men in Leicester. Meetings were held in the market-place to protest against the measures of the Poor Law Guardians, and against the support afforded to them in their harsh measures by the magistrates. And at these meetings I and my Chartist friends were often speakers . . . At length they resisted one of the officials set to watch them at the wheel and this led to a riot in which the windows of the Union Poor House were broken. Police, however, were soon on the spot: the disorder was quelled and the ringleaders taken into custody. The whole affair was utterly unconnected with our Chartist Association. None of the men who were in custody were on our books as members.

Source: Thomas Cooper, *The life of Thomas Cooper*, 1872, reprinted with an introduction by John Saville, Leicester, 1971, pp. 182–84

5.3 Two views from the *Northern Star*

a) Resolution of the Chartist delegates at the Manchester conference, 17 August 1842

That whilst the Chartist body did not originate the present cessation from labour, this Conference of Delegates from various parts of England, express their deep sympathy with their constituents, the working men now on strike; and that we strongly approve the extension and continuance of their present struggle till the PEOPLE'S CHARTER becomes a legislative enactment, and decide forthwith to issue an Address to that effect; and pledge ourselves on our return to our respective localities to give proper direction to the people's efforts.

Source: *Northern Star*, 20 August 1842

b) Report of the Manchester conference

Some, and those the majority, were instructed on the part of their constituents, to disclaim all minor and secondary objects of contention and to declare that their resolution was fixed to uphold the strike on no other ground than as a means to obtain the Charter, for which purpose they were resolved to maintain it to the last extremity. Others, and those principally from Stalybridge and the other localities where the strike began, were instructed that their constituents regarded it as merely a trades' strike, a question of wages and trades' rights . . . Of the eighty-five delegates [a delegate meeting of the trades of Manchester and the surrounding districts], fifty-eight declared for the Charter; seven for making it a trades' contest; nineteen to abide by the decision of the meeting.

Source: *Northern Star*, 20 August 1842

5.4 Max Beer: a Fabian perspective

The month of August, 1842, will always be memorable in the annals of Chartism. It was the month in which the movement attained its zenith. It was the month of the general strike in the northern half of Great Britain and of the subordination of the trade unions to political Chartism. The nation was nearing a social cataclysm. The discontent and determination of the working class reached their highest point. Wages sank in spite of all trade unionist effort to keep them up to the level of 1839. The whole trade unionism appeared to the working class to be Sisyphean [futile] labour. Chartist speakers were able at that time to declare, without fear of contradiction or disapproval, in public meetings of trade unionists that economic action had proven utterly ineffective, and that the salvation of the people entirely depended on the passing of the Charter into law or on political power . . . A peaceful general strike was an impossibility, for the forces of the government would make an attempt to suppress and to persecute the strikers, and this could only be countered by the armed opposition of the people. The Chartists must now mobilise the masses of the people and render them irresistible . . . Was the position they adopted the right one? Does it justify the conclusion that the Chartist leaders understood the significance of the situation? Let us examine the state of affairs. The industrial and commercial centres of the Midlands and the North of England were in a state of insurrection; Scotland, Wales and London could easily be mobilised, no longer for purely trade unionist purposes, but in support of the Chartist programme. The trade unions, the operatives, the working men of the whole country followed the standard of Chartism. What was, under these circumstances, O'Connor's duty and that of his lieutenants? Their duty was to take over supreme command . . . But what did the leader do? Absolutely nothing. He left all initiative to the people and returned to London. The throwing down of his weapons can only be interpreted as indicating that he foresaw the failure of the general strike.

Source: Max Beer, *A history of British socialism*, vol. 2, London, 1929, pp. 139, 147, 149

5.5 F. C. Mather: a recent historian's view

Inasmuch as the trade delegates in Manchester endeavoured to rise to their responsibilities it would be difficult to maintain that the general strike for the People's Charter failed for want of leadership. Why, then, did it fail? There are three main reasons. Firstly, it failed because it was bound to fail. The timescale was against it. In a society less artificial than our own, the mere suspension of labour by the industrial working class could not subdue the government in less time than it would take to reduce the strikers by starvation . . . The general strike for the People's Charter failed secondly because it lacked sufficient support from workers in the basic industries. This is sometimes obscured by the fact that the conference of trade delegates had so large a majority in favour of it . . . More than half of those present on August 15th came from what is loosely designated the aristocracy of labour: the unrevolutionised skilled handicrafts and the mechanical and engineering trades. Out in the country, in the mill towns about Manchester, nothing like a firm consensus for adopting the Charter developed at any stage of the outbreak. Some towns like Hyde and Glossop declared enthusiastically for a Chartist strike; others such as Stockport, Macclesfield, Stalybridge, Mossley, Lees and Bury remained basically in favour of keeping to a demand for higher wages . . . The divisions within the working classes cannot be easily explained. They were often more a matter of locality than of occupation. It is, nevertheless, clear that the proposal to abstain from work until the People's Charter became the law of the land was not endorsed by the workmen in some important sectors of British industry . . . Finally, the strike failed because of the action taken by the government to restore order. This was swift and determined, more vigorous perhaps than that of any government since Lord Sidmouth was at the Home Office. It quickly removed the leaders, demoralised the participants in the turnout mobs and created a framework of stability within which a return to work could and did commence.

Source: F. C. Mather, 'The general strike of 1842', in John Stevenson and Roland Quinault (eds.), *Popular protest and public order*, London, 1974, pp. 132–35.

5.6 James Epstein: a revisionist perspective

The strike for the Charter quickly faded; workers who remained out on strike by late August generally had reverted to wage demands. Given the lack of centralised planning and co-ordination, the arrest of most of the trades and Chartist leaders, the confusion within the ranks of the strikers themselves over the objects of their action and the localised nature of the conflict, the failure to mobilise and sustain a national strike for the Charter is hardly surprising. Summer 1842 witnessed a massive eruption of class tensions, underpinned by widespread working-class aspirations for fundamental social and political change. The class lines were drawn with extraordinary sharpness. Furthermore, the Chartist movement achieved something which it had failed to achieve in 1839, the official backing of large and significant sections of the trade-union movement. What was lacking was the extensive period of preparation which had characterised the 1839 challenge and the concentration of national attention upon the decisions of the Convention. The expectations which had prevailed in 1839, the sense that the country was on the brink of a decisive confrontation between the people and their corrupt rulers, had receded in the early 1840s; there was little talk of arming the people . . . In 1842 Chartism faced a dual crisis. On the one hand, the movement had to define its orientation towards middle-class radicalism, in particular to the CSU; on the other hand, the movement had to respond to the strikes of the summer at a time when the Chartist leadership had retreated from the confrontationalism of 1839 . . . Strategically the movement had reached an impasse . . . The strikes of 1842 had important repercussions for the course of Chartism and the definition of class relations in the 1840s . . . However, the long-range effect of the strikes may have been somewhat different, contributing to a shift in the ruling-class response to the working-class movement . . . In terms of government social policy, there was a curbing of the aggressive thrust of the 1830s – extended factory legislation, a relaxed Poor Law, measures to promote education and urban improvement . . . It seems likely that the erosion of Chartism's mass presence in the mid-1840s more clearly reflected a shift of emphasis from within the working-class movement itself; a shift linked to the failure of Chartist strategy in 1839 and 1842, but also indicative of a gradual coming to terms with industrial capitalism.

Source: James Epstein, *The lion of freedom: Feargus O'Connor and the Chartist movement, 1832–1842*, London, 1982, pp. 297–99

Document case-study questions

1 How far does 5.1 reflect contemporary views that the Chartists exploited the summer strikes of 1842?

2 To what extent do 5.2 and 5.3 support the conclusions of 5.1, and in what ways do they differ?

3 5.4 talks of 'the subordination of the trade unions to political Chartism'. How far do you think Max Beer sustains the case for this conclusion?

4 Why did the strikes fail in 1842? What conclusions does F. C. Mather come to in 5.5?

5 In what respects do the conclusions of 5.5 support the notion of strikes hijacked by Chartists put forward in 5.1, 5.2, 5.3 and 5.4?

6 How do the reasons given for the failure of the strikes in 5.5 differ from those in 5.6?

7 5.6 provides a detailed explanation for the significance of the events of 1842 to the Chartist movement. How convincing do you find James Epstein's conclusions?

8 'The main problem facing the Chartist leadership in general, and O'Connor in particular, was that it was reacting to situations rather than creating them. This, above all, accounts for the failure of Chartism in 1842.' Discuss.

Notes and references

1 *Northern Star*, 3 April 1841.

2 D. A. Hamer, *The politics of electoral pressure: a study in the history of Victorian reform agitations*, Brighton, 1977, especially pp. 9–37.

3 Joel Wiener, *William Lovett*, Manchester, 1989, pp. 76–95, gives the clearest account of Lovett's role in the period from 1840 to 1842.

4 William Lovett and John Collins, *Chartism: a new organisation of the people*, 1840, Leicester, reprinted in Leicester in 1969 with an introduction by Asa Briggs.

5 David Goodway, *London Chartism, 1838–1848*, Cambridge, 1982, pp. 40–42.

6 James Epstein, *The lion of freedom: Feargus O'Connor and the Chartist movement, 1832–1842*, London, 1982, pp. 236–49.

7 William Lovett, *The life and struggles of William Lovett in pursuit of bread, knowledge and freedom*, London, 1876, pp. 202–7, Fitzroy edn, London, 1967.

8 H. U. Faulkner, *Chartism and the churches: a study in democracy*, New York, 1916, is still, despite its age, perhaps the best introduction to the subject. It should, however, be supplemented by more recent work, especially E. Yeo, 'Christianity in Chartist struggle, 1838–1842', *Past and Present*, vol. 91 (1981).

9 On Chartism in Scotland, see Alexander Wilson, *The Chartist movement in Scotland*, Manchester, 1970, and Alexander Wilson, 'Chartism in Glasgow', in Asa Briggs, *Chartist studies*, London, 1959. W. H. Fraser, 'The Scottish context of Chartism', in Terry Brotherstone (ed.), *Covenant, Charter and party: traditions of revolt and protest in modern Scottish history*, Aberdeen, 1989, looks at the subject in the light of recent research.

10 Valuable biographical information on O'Neill can be found in Joyce M. Bellamy and John Saville (ed.), *Dictionary of labour biography*, vol. 6, London, 1982.

11 *Scottish Patriot*, quoted in Wilson, *The Chartist movement*, p. 145.

12 R. F. Wearmouth, *Methodism and the working-class movements of England, 1800–1850*, London, 1937, pp. 138–63.

13 Brian Harrison, *Drink and the Victorians*, London, 1971, revised edition Keele, 1994, is the seminal work on the nineteenth-century temperance movement. His 'Teetotal Chartism', *History*, vol. 58 (June 1973), provides the basis for this section.

14 Harrison, 'Teetotal Chartism', p. 196.

15 *True Scotsman*, 16 May 1840, quoted in Harrison, 'Teetotal Chartism', p. 197.

16 On Vincent, see Bellamy and Saville (eds.), *Dictionary of labour biography*, vol. 1.

17 O'Connor was not alone in this: Richard Cobden took a similar line with the Anti-Corn Law League.

18 *Northern Star*, 10 October 1846.

19 *Northern Star*, 13 March 1841.

20 Derek Fraser, *Urban politics in Victorian England*, Leicester, 1976, and *Power and authority in the Victorian city*, Oxford, 1979, provide the best contexts. J. Garrard, *Leadership and power in Victorian industrial towns, 1830–1850*, Manchester, 1983, considers the municipal context of Chartism in Rochdale, Bolton and Salford.

21 J. F. C. Harrison, 'Chartism in Leeds', in A. Briggs, *Chartist studies*, London, 1959, pp. 65–98, is a useful starting point but, as Fraser, in *Urban politics*, p. 257, points out, his study is 'marred by errors and omissions'.

22 From the mid-eighteenth century, towns had set up bodies for lighting and draining the streets and also for scavenging and watching. These bodies were collectively known as the improvement commission, which was the main agency for sanitary reform. In Leeds the rate-payers elected commissioners.

23 Mark Hovell, *The Chartist movement*, Manchester, 2nd edn, 1925, p. 196.

24 Epstein, *The lion of freedom*, p. 225, suggests that political historians have tended to see the Anti-Corn Law League as the model of Victorian extra-parliamentary political organisation and have tended to ignore the considerable and 'much more ambitious' achievement of the NCA. He makes a compelling case. However, he neglects to mention the seminal role played by the anti-slavery movement, from which all extra-parliamentary pressure groups drew their inspiration.

25 The Corresponding Societies Act, 1799 provided the basis for this concern. Albert Goodwin, *The friends of liberty*, London, 1979, pp. 451–99, provides the context.

26 *British Statesman*, 5 November 1842.

27 *Northern Star*, 28 March 1840.

28 On the LPRA, see Epstein, *The lion of freedom*, pp. 265–73 and Fraser, *Urban politics*, pp. 260–61.

29 On the Complete Suffrage Union, Epstein, *The lion of freedom*, pp. 286–302, gives the best examination of Chartist responses. Alexander Wilson, 'The suffrage movement', in P. Hollis (ed.), *Pressure from without in early Victorian England*, London, 1974, considers the 1840s and the 1850s with a useful section on the CSU. Alex Tyrrell, *Joseph Sturge and the Moral Radical Party in early Victorian Britain*, London, 1987, is the standard biography.

30 The defeat of the Whig administration in the general election of 1841 and its replacement with the Conservative administration of Sir Robert Peel posed problems for both the Anti-Corn Law League and Chartism. The Conservatives, especially the Tory wing of the party, had opposed the Whig constitutional reforms and were in favour of retaining the Corn Law.

31 Mick Jenkins, *The general strike of 1842*, London, 1980, surveys the wave of strikes with a particular emphasis on Lancashire.

6 Chartism: phase 3, 1843–48

The year 1842 may have been that of Chartism, as Dorothy Thompson suggests, but it was also the year from which Chartism would not recover.[1] Popular radicalism would not be extinguished, but the strike of 1842 was the last occasion when the working class would mount an effective, potentially revolutionary, challenge to the ruling establishment. Mainstream politicians would not agree to the Charter, as the subsequent events of 1848 clearly demonstrated, but Peel, and then Russell, made increasing concessions to its social demands. A process of 'liberalisation' had begun; its extent is open to doubt, but it was enough to lead to Chartism losing much of its resonance and appeal.

With the notable exceptions of the Land Plan and the dramatic events of 1848, the third phase of Chartism has received less attention from historians than its two earlier stages.[2] In part, the reasons for this neglect are straightforward: after 1842, there were fewer confrontations with authority; the tendency, which was evident in 1841 and 1842, for Chartism to become fragmented became more pronounced, and it became divided into a number of different movements. The dearth of historical analysis of this period is nonetheless surprising. Was Chartism, as J. T. Ward suggests,[3] now 'entering a period of decline'? Had it been weakened by 'O'Connor's regular arguments and bullying tactics'? Was it 'further weakened by a slow but general economic improvement'?

O'Connorite radicalism, 1843–46: a Chartist rump?

By the end of 1842, O'Connor's pre-eminence within the Chartist movement was complete. Real or potential rivals to O'Connor were either, like Lovett, involved in alternative, working-class self-help schemes or, like the increasingly sceptical Cooper, about to be imprisoned. An increasingly negative view of O'Connor, which was actively sponsored by Lovett and Vincent and then reiterated by Gammage during the 1850s, began to emerge, and this view found expression in much historical writing until quite recently. Ward, for example, said: 'What was left of organised Chartism was now controlled by the megalomaniac Irishman' and that he 'was now the monarch of a declining kingdom'.[4] In many respects, it is difficult to disagree with this view: O'Connor had converted the Chartist rump into a personal following in a way that was not the case before 1842.

The Land Plan dominated the four years after 1843.[5] O'Connor had hinted at its implementation as early as July 1840, and he raised it again at the 1842

Chartist Convention. However, in April 1843 he faced another problem when he and 58 northern Chartists and strike leaders were tried for seditious conspiracy. The results of the trials were a triumph for the movement: although 16 men were convicted of using threatening language, and a further 15, including O'Connor,

THE MODERN MILO.

What point is the cartoonist making about Feargus O'Connor's predicament in this *Punch* cartoon of 1842? (Milo was a legendary Greek wrestler famous for his great strength. In his efforts to tear a tree in two, he became caught in the cleft and was eaten alive by wolves.)

were found guilty of encouraging a strike, they were released on a legal technicality.[6] O'Connor now turned to repositioning Chartism. There was a growing shift in the political and economic agendas that shaped the radical discourse: the mass platform remained strong, but its importance was being increasingly eclipsed by an economic critique that was based on the division between capital and labour. The arguments of the 'labour question' appealed to the working class, which had first-hand experience of it, and substantial owners of capital, especially factory owners, became increasingly subject to attack in the pages of the *Northern Star*. The language used by O'Connor and other Chartists – 'the steam aristocracy' (factory owners), 'the aristocracy of capital' – may have reflected traditional rhetoric, but the focus of the Chartist argument was changing. John Belchem[7] suggests that the rigidity of its public political language undermined Chartism far more than the changing social and economic conditions. The Charter alone offered working people real protection against uncontrolled capitalism. It was against this background that O'Connor proposed the Land Plan. The call for a return to the land, O'Connor argued, would both increase agricultural productivity and extend workers' personal independence; above all, it might counter the growing dominance of machinery and appeal to his declining working-class constituency.[8] Chartism, despite its diversity, contained a distinctive anti-machinery element and corresponding rhetoric. The Land Plan expressed O'Connor's passionate dislike, not for technological innovations as such, but for the results of the Industrial Revolution for working people. It was now necessary to convince the NCA of his beliefs.

NCA activity, together with the *Northern Star*'s circulation figures, declined during 1843, reflecting the growing disenchantment with the movement following the failures of 1842. The *Northern Star* attacked opposition to Graham's Factory Bill of 1843 (which proposed improvements in factory conditions but was vehemently opposed by nonconformists over its 'education clauses' that would have given the Church of England control over factory schools). Some Chartists, led by Harney,[9] Doyle and West, called for closer links between Chartism and O'Connell's campaign to repeal the 1800 Act of Union which had made Ireland part of Great Britain. A convention, planned for April, finally met in Birmingham in early September. Its 30 members met for four days in order to reconstruct the NCA. O'Connor dominated the proceedings, and the outcome was much as he suggested. The reorganised NCA, not surprisingly, accepted O'Connor's Land Plan. The post of general secretary of the NCA was offered to Lovett in a vain attempt to reunite the movement. He declined; the breach with O'Connor was unbridgeable. After the convention, O'Connor headed north, intending to revitalise Chartist ardour, but instead finding that Scottish Chartism was disintegrating: some Chartist churches remained, but radicals were now more concerned with causes like temperance, sanitary reform, factory reform and poor relief. Scottish interest in the Land Plan and in Chartist unity based on the NCA flickered, but did little more; only the Dumfries Working Men's Association joined the NCA and the Glasgow Charter Association held aloof until the following year.

Chartism appeared sluggish during 1844. The economy continued to improve, thus draining support from the movement. The final form of the NCA was agreed at a convention held in Manchester in April, but the delegates refused to ratify the Land Plan, with most members arguing for separation between the NCA and the scheme. The ailing *Northern Star* moved to London. The haemorrhage of Chartists from the national movement continued. O'Connor was, however, determined to press on with the Land Plan and also hoped for a trade-union alliance. His attitude to unions during the early 1840s was ambivalent: he had little faith in the unions that had so regularly rejected his leadership, and that had shown a lack of interest in the fate of the leaders of the Newport Rising; by 1845, however, he needed allies, and this led to a short-lived change of attitude that was reflected in his new journal, *The Northern Star and National Trades Journal*. Some miners' groups supported the move for an alliance, and O'Connor's friend, the MP Thomas Slingsby Duncombe, was made president of the National Association of United Trades for the Protection of Labour when it was formed in March 1845.[10] Most unions, however, remained aloof, and O'Connor quickly reverted to his old attitude towards them. The alliance failed because the appeal of Chartism to trade unions had already been undermined by the shift towards 'respectability'. There was also a growing pluralism and increasing competition between the proposers of 'new-model' forms of working-class culture; affiliated friendly societies, amalgamated trade unions and retail co-operative societies all had what the NCA lacked: public approval and legal recognition.[11] The Land Plan was an attempt to reverse this pluralistic trend.

The 1845 Chartist convention met at the London Parthenium on 21 April; only 14 delegates attended it. When O'Connor unveiled the details of his Land Plan the following day, they were enthusiastic and resolved to set up the Chartist Land Society, which was eventually founded on 19 May. In retrospect, O'Connor may have been deluded about the financial viability and ultimate practicality of the scheme, but his judgement on its potential appeal was flawless. Despite opposition from Cooper and O'Brien, support for it grew. This enthusiasm was greatest in the Lancashire cotton towns, and was becoming stronger in London, the north-east, the Midlands and Yorkshire; only Scotland and Wales proved difficult to rouse. In December, a convention was held in Manchester solely to consider the Land Plan, and here O'Connor dropped his long-standing opposition to the Anti-Corn Law League.

From early 1840, the Chartists had generally been opposed to the Anti-Corn Law League.[12] There was suspicion on both sides. For Chartists, the League, with its single, overriding objective to have the Corn Laws repealed, reflected middle-class attitudes and a free-trade ideology. In 1841, O'Connor advised his followers to vote Tory, thus ranging him against the free-trade measures that were put forward by the Whigs in the 1841 budget. During its early years, the League hoped for substantial working-class support, but it had little need to show direct interest in Chartism: to achieve repeal, the League needed either to persuade a majority in the House of Commons to vote for it, or to stir up the electorate to such an extent that it would only accept candidates who were committed to repeal and, as the working classes were not generally voters, their political support could not be of direct help in either of these aims.

Lucy Brown identified two phases in the relationship between Chartism and the League. Between 1840 and 1842 there were attempts, both locally and nationally, to find common ground between the two organisations. Although the League had some success in co-operating with the Chartists, especially in Wolverhampton and Sheffield, this was very limited. The events of 1842, especially the strikes, destroyed any hope of class reconciliation and resulted in increasing antagonism between O'Connor and the League. Growing economic prosperity between 1843 and 1845, however, helped to soothe the Chartists' fears of repeal and led to a gradual softening of their attitudes towards the League. O'Connor continued to attack the 'mountebank [fake] cosmopolites' who saw free trade as the solution to all society's ills, but his growing interest in agricultural matters caused a change in his attitude to both Richard Cobden, the League's leader, and Peel, the Tory prime minister, between 1844 and 1845, and he increasingly came to support the case for repeal. Gammage was highly critical of this change in policy: 'We ask, Was not his whole opposition to the League a mere sham?'[13] His judgement is harsh.[14] The years between 1845 and 1851 saw a 'mid-century crisis'[15] and O'Connor was not unique in recognising the 'spirit of the age' in late 1845 and early 1846: he saw where events were heading and changed tack. His strategy paid off: in July 1846, he was elected MP for Nottingham in a by-election.

The Land Plan

Although the Chartist Land Plan formed a central plank of Chartist activities during the mid and late 1840s, it has attracted little attention from recent historians[16] and appears to have passed revisionist historians by (Epstein's biography, for example, stopped short of considering it in depth). The idea was to raise capital for a land company by selling shares priced at 3d (pence) or more a week to ordinary people. Land would then be bought and made into small-holdings. Shareholders, chosen by ballot, would rent the land. The income thus received would fund the purchase of further estates. Much of what modern thinking there is on the Land Plan has been coloured by contemporary hostility to O'Connor: Gammage was damning in his critique of the scheme[17] and subsequent historians were quick to view it as either an irrelevance or as an unwarranted diversion from the campaign for the Charter.[18] Recent historians have been nearly as uncharitable, dismissing it as 'unquestionably reactionary' and 'harebrained',[19] 'Utopian', 'nostalgic' and 'escapist'.[20] Malcolm Chase rightly argues that the Land Plan has been the victim of a 'Whig interpretation', with the result that the Land Plan was dismissed as being a cul-de-sac.

One aspect of the Land Plan has been subject to considerable revision during the last 20 years, however, and this is O'Connor's association with it. While it is possible to look at Chartism as a whole without including O'Connor, his role in the Land Plan was so fundamental that without him, as Chase says, 'the Land

Plan would [have] be[en] inconceivable'.[21] The 'land question' had been at the heart of the radical agenda since the late eighteenth century[22] and the 1830s and 1840s saw a widespread interest in schemes that were designed to settle workers on the land. O'Connor consciously built on this interest. His recognition of the importance of land contained two, in part contradictory, analyses. Firstly, he wanted to re-establish a balance between industry and agriculture; like William Cobbett, he drew an idealised and highly moralised portrait of a rural 'golden age' with its 'cottage economy'. He was not opposed to machinery as such, but to the consequence of its use in factories: the displacement of workers and the unequal distribution of the wealth thereby created. Secondly, and more importantly, O'Connor wanted to establish communities that were based upon the independence of the worker, and he saw the land as a means of providing comfort and security for working people. This view went to the heart of Chartist demands and gave the movement renewed momentum after the debacle of 1842. The widening divisions in society, many believed, were driving it to the brink of disaster. O'Connor, as Epstein says,[23] was not advancing any original economic or social ideas; however, he did capture an 'artisan consciousness concerned with the values of independence and self-reliance'. Whether Epstein is right in saying that this was a '"backward-looking" ideal in the sense that it implied an arresting of the full development of the emergent forces of industrial capitalism' is, however, more debatable.

Local Chartists readily took up O'Connor's call for local 'Chartist land associations' as early as August 1840; Cirencester – a decaying textile centre – was the first locality to consider forming a land association. Such provincial support finally secured official Chartist approval for the Land Plan at the Birmingham convention in 1843. Certainly, the Land Plan revitalised the movement and provided a major outlet for the frustrations of certain Chartists. It proved immensely popular, but also provided an opportunity for their opponents to heap further ridicule upon them. What distinguished the Land Plan was its large size, which had never been anticipated and which helps to explain its ultimate failure. At its peak, it attracted some 70,000 weekly subscribers. Initial support for it came from the industrial north and the Midlands, but enthusiasm soon spread south. The national list of subscribers for 1847 to 1848 is an invaluable, but neglected, source for historians studying the later phase of Chartism.[24] Evidence from a sample of 171 Liverpool subscribers[25] shows that skilled workers, tailors and stonemasons made up 60 per cent of the total, and that there was an almost complete absence of unskilled or semi-skilled workers, like dockers, warehousemen and seamen.

The Land Plan's momentum gathered after O'Connor had purchased his first site near Watford, and on May Day 1847 the first tenants moved into 'O'Connorville'. Subscriptions soared, and the renamed National Co-operative Land Company bought further estates in Worcestershire at Lowbands, Snigs End, Minster Lovell and Great Dodford. Over £100,000 was raised, although only 250 of the 70,000 subscribers ever settled on the two-acre allotments. Despite the sum raised, however, the company and its associated Land Bank were plagued by legal difficulties.[26] Furthermore, in May 1848, following concerns about O'Connor's role in the scheme, parliament appointed a select committee to investigate the National Co-operative Land Company; although it found no evidence to justify the rumours of fraud, the company's accounts were confused and inaccurate and this further weakened confidence in the scheme. O'Connor found that the flow of share capital was drying up and, after exploring alternative means of saving the scheme, finally took the route recommended by the select committee and wound up the company in 1851.

It is not enough to blame the collapse of the Land Plan on the breakdown of O'Connor's health and personal finances, as well as on his declining authority within the movement after 1848. Government obstruction and the sheer impracticality of the scheme also played their part. The collapse of the Land Plan may have marked the end of agrarian fundamentalism, but the appeal of going 'back to the land' remained strong and interest in the 'land question' continued into the 1850s. The Chartist Convention of 1851, for example, accepted land nationalisation as a central aspect of its political programme, while Ernest Jones[27] and his supporters embraced agrarian reform in the labour parliament (an institution recommended enthusiastically a decade before by O'Connor) between 1853 and 1854. Popular belief in land reform as a way of ensuring the prosperity of the working class endured.

Alternative directions, 1843–48

Earlier historians, especially Mark Hovell and Julius West, gave the impression that the Chartist movement after 1842 lacked ideas or activities apart from the Land Plan. This was far from being the case, however. Some Chartists established links with European revolutionaries through such organisations as the Society of Fraternal Democrats and the People's International League. Others turned to the registration of electors (thus to ensure that any working man entitled to vote was on the electoral register) as a way of building up Chartist support in parliament. Some returned to a revived factory-reform movement in 1846. The proposed reorganisation of the militia by the government led to Chartist involvement in the National Anti-Militia Association under the slogan 'No vote, no musket'. Still others turned to socialism. This section briefly considers three important themes:

1 the issue of English and Irish radicalism;
2 the question of internationalism;
3 the relationship between socialism and Chartism.

English and Irish radicalism
The alliance between English radicalism and Irish nationalism dates from the 1790s. Demands for the repeal of the 1800 Act of Union were common at English working-class meetings, and the radical unstamped press gave substantial coverage to Irish issues during the early 1830s. There was already a large and growing Irish population in England which was concentrated throughout the industrial north and in London. Irish affairs, especially the repeal of the Act of

Union and opposition to governmental coercion, played a central part in radical thinking during the 1830s and 1840s. O'Connor's appeals for social justice for Ireland during this period were closely linked with his calls for justice for English workers. However, there was conflict over work and religion between Irish workers and Chartists in Manchester in 1841 and 1842, while Irish opposition to Chartism in other areas drew workers away from becoming involved in Chartism. Epstein argues that 'the fragmentation within sections of the northern industrial working class, between Irish and English workers, was a source of Chartist weakness'.[28]

It is difficult to calculate the level of Irish support for O'Connor and the Chartist movement.[29] Traditional studies have tended to focus on the antagonistic relationship between Daniel O'Connell, who led the demands for the repeal of the Act of Union during the 1830s and 1840s, and O'Connor. O'Connell saw Chartism as a potential threat to his campaign and, along with the Catholic Church, sought to minimise Irish support for the movement. Irish immigrants remained aloof from Chartism because of the policy of O'Connell and the leaders of the Irish associations, as well as the critical attitude of the Catholic clergy towards the movement.[30] There was no formal link between Irish nationalism and Chartism until after 1847; J. H. Treble took the view that it was not until 1848 that the 'vast majority' of Irish people in the northern industrial counties had any significant contact with Chartism. Dorothy Thompson, by contrast, has shown that informal co-operation between Chartists and Irish workers was common, especially in the smaller manufacturing towns and villages before 1848. However, the events of 1848 were different in several respects from anything that had happened earlier, and Treble was right to emphasise this.

Important shifts took place among the Irish leadership following O'Connell's death in mid-1847. The Irish Democratic Federation, founded in London between August and September 1847, campaigned for the repeal of the Act of Union. In addition, the ideas of the Irish radical, Fintan Lalor, on land and political reform had an important influence on the policies of the revolutionary Young Ireland movement from early 1847.[31] His policy of social radicalism was further invigorated by the news of the success of the many revolutions in Europe in 1848. Finally, O'Connor made a vigorous attack on the Crimes and Outrages Bill (which proposed increasing the repression of Ireland) in the House of Commons. These developments all helped to create a new understanding between the Chartists and Irish radicals, and provided the basis for an informal, but firm, agreement of mutual support between the Irish Confederation of radicals and the Chartists. It is significant that the major centres of Chartist activity in 1848 – London, Bradford and the West Riding, Manchester and its surrounding towns, and Liverpool – were precisely those towns and regions where there was a concentration of Irish immigrants.

These developments posed problems for the government: in 1839 and, to a lesser extent in 1842, Ireland had been relatively quiet, and this allowed the government to move troops from Ireland to the British mainland; in 1847 and 1848 this was not the case. It would appear that the alliance was having an effect. There was, however, one important difference between the Chartists and the Irish radicals: the Chartists were essentially constitutional in their approach, while the Irish in England were no longer restrained by O'Connell's proscription of physical force. This placed a great strain on the Chartist–Irish alliance. The Kennington Common meeting of 10 April 1848 was followed by violent confrontations between the police and radicals in early June, and by the plans of a small group of London Chartists and confederates for a rising on 16 August. It is clear that the Chartists failed to exploit the full revolutionary possibilities of their alliance with the Irish.

John Belchem argues that radical Anglo-Irish co-operation in 1847 and 1848 did not strengthen the working-class challenge to the establishment of early Victorian England. Indeed, in many respects, it helped the government more than the Chartists. The establishment press exploited the Irish question as often as it could: *The Times* commented on 10 April that 'The Repealers wish to make as great a hell of this island as they have made of their own'; *Punch* pictured the Chartists revelling in rape, pillage and massacre. There is ample evidence of the distrust of, and antagonism towards, Irish immigrants during this period and racial and religious prejudice formed an important part of the social consciousness of the majority of the ordinary people who took little or no part in the events of 1848. Radical Anglo-Irish political solidarity during the late 1840s gave way to anti-Irish riots during the 1850s and 1860s.

The question of internationalism

Chartism was a remarkably insular movement, which was suspicious of foreign and colonial causes because they tended to deflect attention from the Charter and the Land Plan.[32] O'Connor, Peter McDouall (a leading London Chartist) and Bronterre O'Brien were the leading advocates of the view that Britain was suffering perhaps the worst form of despotism in Europe, and that priority should be given to the rights of the English working class. Russia was regarded as one of the major threats to the stability and peace of Europe, and fear of Russian aggression was an important feature of the 1830s and 1840s; a critical figure in fanning these fears was David Urquhart.[33] Urquhart, as a diplomat in Constantinople (now Istanbul) during the early 1830s, developed an almost paranoid fear that Russia was seeking to dominate the Near East. His dismissal in 1837 inflamed his Russophobia to such an extent that he believed that Russian gold and influence had penetrated to the heart of British policy. The anti-Whig flavour of his campaign and his appeal to patriotism led to some Chartists supporting him in 1839 and 1840. William Cardo, a Marylebone shoemaker, Robert Lowery and John Warden of Bolton, for example, formed the core of a Chartist 'foreign-policy' group, which put the immediate threat of Russian domination before the long-term objectives of the Charter, and gained the support of the Chartist newspaper, the *Northern Liberator*. In late 1840, however, O'Connor attacked the *Northern Liberator* and the 'wild goose-chase' of 'Foreign Policy Chartists' and the new movement collapsed. He also attacked George Julian Harney and Ernest Jones for their alleged fixation on foreign affairs later in the 1840s, but to less effect. There was, moreover, a second dimension to O'Connor's attitudes: he was intensely suspicious of middle-class collaboration. Indeed, it was middle-class radicals like Urquhart, the Reverend Edward Miall (who was committed to the separation of church and state) and Sturge who dominated the 'foreign-policy' group.

During the early years of the movement, some Chartists were extremely interested in foreign policy. This was paralleled by an intense suspicion of the foreign policies of successive British governments: the Chartists regarded the war scares of 1840 to 1841, 1844, 1846 and 1848 either as follies, or as attempts to divert attention from their movement. Britain's support for what the Chartists considered the 'corrupt monarchies and priesthoods' of Europe was also criticised and the visit to England of Tsar Nicholas in 1844 led to widespread Chartist protest. Colonial policy was also denounced, for maladministration and brutality in the colonies had their parallels in Britain. Larger Chartist associations in Nottingham, Newcastle, south London, Todmorden and Sheffield had 'international committees'. Internationalist addresses, like those contained in Lovett's autobiography, as well as émigré funds, testify to Chartists' awareness of international issues and their sense of international responsibility. By the late 1840s, those who feared Chartist violence frequently associated it with revolutions abroad.

Hetherington and Lovett pioneered the view that Chartism was an integral part of a wider European movement for working-class freedom: in 1844, for example, Lovett formed the Democratic Friends of All Nations that merged into the People's International League in 1847.[34] Lovett often took a more aggressive stance against instances of foreign oppression than his reputation as a moderate would suggest. In a series of LWMA addresses beginning in the mid-1830s, Lovett developed militant and increasingly pacifist ideas. The world, he argued, would be a safer place in which social and political reform could be effected if all sources of human conflict were removed. He saw the world as being organised along the lines of nationality and fused this view with his advocation of class solidarity and non-violent resistance. He sought 'freedom, peace and brotherhood'. Lovett was highly critical of the Society of Fraternal Democrats (founded in 1845), which became the principal organ of the class-conscious internationalism of the Chartist left, including principally Jones and Harney. They saw internationalism not as an end in itself, but as an intermediate step on the path to international revolution and took a more aggressive approach, the result of the active involvement in the organisation of exiled continental revolutionaries living in London. The Society of Fraternal Democrats exerted limited influence on Chartism except during the excitement raised by the 1848 revolutions.[35] The subsequent repression of the revolutionaries in France did not dent Jones and Harney's belief in the need for a true social revolution and during the 1850s they continued to educate the British people about the realities of political conditions in Europe through papers like the *Democratic Review* and the *Red Republican*.

John Saville locates the radical challenge of 1848 'within the triangle of revolutionary Paris, insurgent Ireland and a revitalised native Chartist movement in London and the industrial North'.[36] Shared enthusiasm for the French February revolution, he argues, served to unite Chartists and Irish nationalists throughout the United Kingdom. In addition, many Chartists joined middle-class liberals in demonstrations in favour of European revolutionaries like Kossuth and Garibaldi. Others, like Jones, Harney and O'Brien, became involved in the social-democratic organisations that dominated radical internationalism in the 1850s.

The relationship between socialism and Chartism

Robert Owen (1771–1858) developed his socialist ideology after a successful career as a factory owner. He believed that a 'new moral order' could be created, based not on the competition of the capitalist system, but on co-operation between workers. Gregory Claeys argues in his study of early British socialism that any 'study of the relations between Owenism and Chartism is hampered by a variety of obstacles'.[37] Not least of these is the unsystematic way in which historians have treated the Owenite–Chartist links.[38] Gammage had little to say on the subject except in the context of the post-1848 Chartist programme. Mark Hovell argued that only a few Chartists were 'downright Socialists', the majority discounting Owen because of his belief in communitarian equality. Julius West, by contrast, argued in 1920 that Chartism was 'permeated with Socialist ideas' because of Chartist support for state intervention in the economy. Some local studies have extended our understanding of the links between Owenites and Chartists, while many others simply fail to mention the connection at all.

There was much in common between the early socialists and Chartists:[39] they broadly agreed on the devastation of rural life and the alienation and distress caused by the new capitalist society. Some people chose to belong to both camps and David Jones gives three examples: Isaac Ironside of Sheffield; John Goodwyn Barnby, a poet and 'communist'; and Thomas Liversey, a Chartist leader and treasurer of the Rochdale Owenite Institution.[40] However, conflict between the two groups was perhaps inevitable. The Chartists were, for example, generally less bold in their analysis of existing society and their vision of the new; for Owenites, the Chartist programme was 'crude and undigested'. They also disagreed about method. Unlike many Chartists, Owen rejected political action and threats of violence. The Chartist press vigorously denounced the Owenites on various grounds, thus creating tensions on both sides: it attacked the Owenites' antipathy to religion ('Christian Chartists' took their beliefs seriously). It further argued that socialism had been tried and had failed. Chartist attitudes to economics varied, but many would have agreed with O'Connor, who stated in 1843 that 'a fair day's wages for a fair day's work was the aim and end of the People's Charter'; communitarian equality, as suggested by Owen, was never part of the Chartist political agenda. Such tension between the two groups was a recurrent problem. During the late 1830s and early 1840s, Owenites often left the Chartist movement on the grounds of its militancy and limited aims: in Leeds, for example, John Bray and the Owenites withdrew from the local working men's association. Owenites complained in Halifax, Bath and Dunfermline that Chartist lecturers distracted people from socialism. Rivalry and even opposition was common, especially since the two movements were often influential in the same areas.

There is ample evidence that, even before 1848, increasing numbers of Chartists were moving towards socialism. The *Northern Star* carried several articles and letters stating that landlords had no intrinsic right to the soil, but only to the implements used on it and the improvements made to it. In early 1847, the Society of Fraternal Democrats became more forthright in its support for land reform and the common ownership of land. At the heart of this move were Bronterre O'Brien – who had argued for land nationalisation since the late 1830s – and the propagandist abilities of Harney. It was, however, the events of 1848 that crystallised much Chartist thinking on socialism. Claeys argues that there were three main reasons for this:[41]

1 The Land Plan was an unlikely agent for social transformation: it was simply too gradual and unwieldy.
2 The Kennington Common meeting of April 1848 and subsequent events between 1848 and 1849 marked the end of 'mass-platform' politics and discredited the Chartist leadership.
3 Chartism ceased to be a narrow, British, political movement, and European socialist ideas became an integral part of British radical thinking.

The result was the acceptance of a largely socialist programme by the Chartist movement in 1851. The significance of this development was that it allowed Chartists, for the first time, to address the question of what would happen *after* the aims of the Charter had been achieved.

1848

For contemporaries like W. E. Adams, and also for later historians, 1848 was a watershed in the history of the Chartist movement.[42] It is certainly true that after 1848 Chartism lost whatever unity it had, with even O'Connor becoming willing to accept household suffrage while leaders such as Jones and Harney moved towards socialism. The winter of 1847 to 1848 was a severe one; the *Northern Star* talked of the 'extreme prevalence' of bronchitis, pneumonia, typhus, measles and scarlatina, and smallpox was also widespread. Neither the commercial crisis of 1847, when the economy slumped, nor the general election of the same year had led to a reinvigorated mass platform, however, and the year of 1848 opened with little prospect of a Chartist revival. The news of the revolutions in Europe reached England in late February 1848, but historians debate whether this revived Chartist spirits. Some regard 1848 as an unnecessary epilogue in the history of a movement that had already been defeated; others view the years between 1848 and 1851 as being important for the welcome infusion of continental social theories and thought that they brought. The authorities feared that the revolutionary spirit sweeping Europe would infect Britain, especially as some Chartists had been in contact with European radicals. Uneasy about Chartist plans to present a third petition, they were also worried that the measures proposed by the Chartist Convention which assembled in London in early April would tie down the army at a time when Irish radicals were threatening rebellion.

In reality, the mass platform had creaked into motion before news of the French revolution reached London.[43] The Chartist Council (the executive) had arranged meetings to promote its new campaign in early January 1848; at the

A PHYSICAL FORCE CHARTIST ARMING FOR THE FIGHT.

What point is the cartoonist trying to make in this 1848 cartoon from *Punch*?

forefront were Jones and Harney. Both recognised that effective organisation and preparation were essential if mass-platform action was to succeed. Jones argued that moral and physical force were 'twin cherries on the stalk . . . by showing a bold physical front, they would prevent the necessity for physical action'.[44] Chartists, Jones continued, needed to develop an organisation that the government would not dare, or be able, to resist; public opinion would triumph. O'Connor's leadership was unquestioned until the rejection of the petition by parliament in April. He remained determined to retain his leadership of the mass platform. O'Connor also called for 'social regeneration' and details of his programme appeared in the *Northern Star* in mid-March. In many respects, this marked a recognition of the redirection of radical activities. O'Connor insisted that the Charter and the land were inseparable. This was, in part, a response to the new language of the 'organisation of labour' that had been initiated by the revolution in France and reflected his belief that the French approach to political and social change was unsuitable for England. At the heart of his argument was his belief that the Land Plan would set 'all the springs of industry at work'.

The appeal to public opinion was a fatal flaw in the arguments of O'Connor, as well as those of Jones and Harney. O'Connor over-estimated middle-class discontent with the Whig government and his appeal for social regeneration made little impression on public opinion. Belchem argues that O'Connor never realised that the 'contest for public opinion had been lost before Kennington Common'.[45] For their part, Jones and Harney could not bring enough discipline and organisation to the mass platform to make it an effective voice for working-class action. Above all, the attitude of the English press was overwhelmingly hostile to the revolution in France and public opinion soon turned in defence of established authority.

London was in the vanguard of the Chartist movement: in March 1848, Chartists took over a middle-class radical meeting in London and demanded the abolition of income tax; attempts by the police to break up the demonstration led to three days of widespread disorder. Similar disturbances took place in Glasgow and Manchester; in each case, although there was an important Chartist presence, looting and other criminal acts were largely perpetrated by petty criminals, but in the eyes of the propertied, Chartism was guilty by association. The Chartist executive tried to set the record straight, but to little effect and Chartist calls for restraint and public order went unheeded. 'Mob' action followed meetings held in Trafalgar Square and, on 13 March, at Kennington Common. The press did not distinguish the Chartists from the criminals, or the revolutionaries from the rioters. Events outside London took a similar form and the Chartists were blamed for various riots in and around workhouses. The local Chartist leadership tried to keep its distance and condemned any criminal behaviour. Middle-class opinion polarised around the need to maintain public order and the lower-middle classes flocked to join the ranks of the special constabulary. The worsening public perception of the Chartist movement was not helped by its increasing identification with Irish agitation. The Irish alliance intensified the Chartist challenge; it may even, as Belchem suggests, 'have strengthened the mass platform'.[46] But this was at a cost: *The Times*, for example, saw Chartism as 'a ramification of the Irish conspiracy'.[47] As the physical strength of the movement grew, its public support evaporated. Under such conditions, the Chartists stood little chance of establishing either the legality of their agitation or the fairness of their demands.

The Chartist Convention was viewed as the key to success. Could it provide central co-ordination and leadership? In short, no. Forty-nine delegates met in London on 4 April. Some, like G. W. M. Reynolds and William Cuffay, were bellicose, at least in their rhetoric; most were not. The programme agreed by the executive was relatively moderate: if the petition was rejected, the convention would address a memorial to Queen Victoria. In the interim, the convention would be dissolved and would be followed by widespread agitation throughout the country, leading to the formation of a more fully representative convention or national assembly. This approach did not appeal to Chartists like Jones, who believed that the convention should immediately declare itself a permanent body, which would both provide clear direction for extra-parliamentary pressure and allow the convention to retain the initiative as the agitation intensified.

The convention planned a peaceful demonstration at Kennington Common for 10 April, followed by a procession to present the petition (which O'Connor hoped would contain 5 million signatures) to parliament. The Whig government was determined to prevent this, however. Public opinion was firmly behind the government and it exploited the increasing hysteria to the full. The Crown and Government Security Bill was now rushed through parliament: this introduced a new charge of felonious sedition, a charge that extended to 'open and advised speaking'. Stuart legislation against 'tumultuous petitioning' was revived to prevent any mass procession through the streets. Strong precautionary measures were taken by the authorities, for whom the Chartist threat was very real: 8,000 troops, for example, were drafted into the capital to support the thousands of special constables. The government was utterly confident and was unwilling to accede to any of the Chartist requests, as a deputation from the convention to the Home Office discovered. For the Chartists, the issue was increasingly whether the meeting should proceed. Bronterre O'Brien had grave doubts about this: he recognised the determination of the government and also the likely effect on public opinion if the meeting went ahead. At secret gatherings with delegates held on 8 and 9 April, Harney called for the meeting and procession to be abandoned. Philip McGrath, as chairman of the convention, sought a last-minute compromise with the commissioners of police. The movement had reached an impasse.

In the event, the procession was banned by the government, but the meeting went ahead. The resolution of the government was sufficient to 'frighten' O'Connor into asking his supporters not to confront the authorities, and to disperse peacefully; the petition was carried to parliament in three cabs, and then the crisis was over. The meeting was ridiculed by many as a 'fiasco', and two days later O'Connor faced further criticism when his claimed five-ton petition was found to weigh barely a quarter of a ton and to contain less than

The absence of women in the crowd is a feature of the earliest photograph of a mass demonstration, taken by William Kilburn at the Great Chartist Meeting, Kennington Common, April 1848.

2 million genuine signatures; this was 'the real "fiasco" of 1848'.[48] In fact, O'Connor regarded the meeting as a decisive moral victory: he had insisted that the meeting went ahead and had ensured that it was peaceful; he had been able to call off the procession without any dissent. As Belchem rightly concludes, he had been able to 'extricate the movement from the difficulty posed by the intractability of the government'.[49] The constitutional right of assembly had been maintained and violence had been avoided.

The convention continued to sit, undaunted by parliament's subsequent rejection of the petition. It organised more mass meetings preparatory to the summoning of a national assembly which would call upon the queen to dissolve parliament and to accept only a government that would be prepared to implement the Charter. Internal disagreement, mutual suspicion and recriminations increasingly paralysed its work, however. O'Connor attacked its handling of the petition, especially with regard to the forged signatures. He was justified in not moving a motion for the Charter. Delegates began to leave London in order to seek guidance in their localities. The convention – although not actually dissolved, as Jones had feared – was rapidly losing the initiative. His hopes that pressure on the government could be maintained through the National Assembly, which met in May, were shattered when O'Connor came out against it on account of the hardening of its views in favour of physical confrontration with the forces of law and order. The few delegates who attended it were as divided over what to do as those to the convention had been, and it collapsed too. This marked the end of Chartist efforts to use the traditional mass platform to obtain the aims of the Charter. However, on 2 June *The Times* concluded that 'Chartism is neither dead nor sleeping. The snake was scotched not killed on the 10th of April. The advancing spring has brought with it warmth, vigour and renovation.'

The spring and summer of 1848 saw a great deal of activity – arrests, trials and several riots – being played out against the background of imminent revolution in Ireland. There was a notable toughening of views among many Chartists, who called for physical confrontation with the forces of the establishment. Was there the potential for a Chartist rising? The focal points of governmental concern in this respect during the summer were Bradford, Manchester, Liverpool and London. Agitation in Manchester began to increase from the middle of May; the most serious problems facing the government during late May and early June, however, came from Bradford and Liverpool. The open drilling of men spread to Leeds and Bingley; Halifax Chartists attended meetings with 'glistening pikes flashing in the sun'. Matters came to a head on 29 May when the botched arrest of two local Chartist leaders led to street violence, which the Bradford police eventually brought under control. *The Times* grudgingly reported that 'if fighting against Special Constables and the police could make a revolution, those who fought at Bradford ought to have succeeded.'[50] It is unclear whether a rising was planned at Bradford at the end of May; whether it was or not, it is unlikely that there was any co-ordinated Chartist action.

There were different levels of preparation for agitation in different towns. Liverpool had remained relatively quiet in April, despite its potential for violence.

Its links with the movement in the rest of the country were weak and its large Irish population appears to have been politically inactive. During May, however, political agitation increased as the result of the growing activity of Irish radicals and the sharpening of politics in Liverpool caused by religious divisions. Social tensions increased in June and July, as did street meetings and incidences of violence. However, vigorous action on the part of the police rapidly restored order, and by early August Liverpool was completely under the control of the forces of law and order. In London, the police broke up meetings in the East End on 4 June, and in response the provisional executive of the National Assembly called a day of protest on 12 June. The government, determined to quash whatever remained of the Chartist threat, replied with a heavy display of force at a meeting held at Bishop Bonner's Field. The hostility of the press and the willingness of the courts to convict Chartist leaders, as well as the rank and file, helped the government's gradual repression of the movement. Chartism soon began to lose its major leaders: Jones was convicted for making a speech at Bishop Bonner's Field; McDouall was brought to trial in late June. The noose of repression was slowly tightened, but encouraged an increased commitment to violence from those Chartists who remained at liberty.

News from Ireland impelled some Chartists towards revolution: first came news of John Mitchel's conviction, then of the suspension of habeas corpus in late July, and finally of Smith O'Brien's abortive rising. Very little of the Irish activity of late July was reported in the *Northern Star*. However, two new papers appeared in Lancashire hoping to direct the outrage at the government's treatment of Ireland into disciplined organisation. The *Truth Teller* called for 'full and perfect organisation' and opposed any idea of planned violence. The *English Patriot and Irish Repealer*, edited by James Leach – a leading Manchester Chartist – put forward a more radical agenda and called for all Irishmen living in England to join an Irish league. Government informers were pessimistic: they detected moves towards maintaining greater secrecy in Irish and Chartist circles, and reported that northern England would rise if there was insurrection – even if it was unsuccessful – in Ireland. The August 'conspiracy' was the government's response: a government informer infiltrated local radical groups in London, as a result of which their leaders were arrested on charges of conspiracy on 16 August. The extent of provincial Chartist involvement in the pro-Irish agitation is more difficult to assess. There is evidence of disagreement between local Chartists and Irish radicals over the use of violence. However, there is much to suggest that Manchester was intended to be the centre of co-ordinated action on either 15 or 16 August. In the event, local magistrates moved first and in a pre-emptive strike arrested 15 Chartist and confederate leaders on the night of 15 August.

Was the Chartist threat real in 1848? To those in authority it certainly was: they saw the daily meetings and riots; they received reports of drilling and military-style marches from the provinces. The events at Kennington Common on 10 April were not seen as marking the end of the movement at the time, nor was it a decisive date. Perhaps the end of the year has a greater claim to that: by then, the leaders of both the Chartist movement and the Irish Confederation were in prison; the National Co-operative Land Company was in difficulty; and the 'year of revolutions' in Europe had ended, not with the creation of just and democratic societies, but with the reassertion of traditional authority. As in 1838 and 1842, Chartism had been contained from without and critically weakened from within. Chartism's failure in 1848 was not one of ideas, but of will. The united mass platform, already weakened, now disintegrated. Chartism as a mass movement was over.

O'Connor and 1848

6.1 Lovett on 1848

A number of us, however, indignant at the efforts made by the Whigs at that time to stifle the reform movement, determined to keep together; to greatly economise our expenditure, and to use every means in our power to keep up the agitation for the suffrage. The Whigs, having effected a triumph over O'Connor and his boasting physical force followers by their blundering demonstration on the 10th of April, and having, moreover, exposed the frauds of fallacies in connection with the 'Monster Petition' presented about that period, resolved to crush, if possible, the right of petitioning altogether. The Government had previously rendered the right of petition nearly a nullity, by preventing members presenting themselves from explaining or supporting them; and now they thought to effectually silence the public voice by raking up an old law of the Stuarts, which declares that political petitions shall not have more than twenty signatures.

Source: William Lovett, *The life and struggles of William Lovett in pursuit of bread, knowledge and freedom*, London, 1876, Fitzroy edn, London, 1967, p. 285

6.2 Thomas Cooper on 1848

Being so thorough separated from O'Connor and his party, I was entirely kept out of the 'Tenth of April' trouble and all the other troubles of the year 1848. I was visited, however, by all sorts of schemers, who wished to draw me into their plots and plans; for plotters and planners were as plentiful as blackberries in 1848. The changes on the Continent seemed to have unhinged the minds of thousands. It was not only among O'Connor Chartists, or Ernest Jones Chartists, and the Irish Repealers, that there were plots, open and secret . . . In the year 1848, I think, Chartists were wilder than we were in 1842 or than the members of the First Convention were in 1848.

Source: Thomas Cooper, *The life of Thomas Cooper*, 1872, reprinted with an introduction by John Saville, Leicester, 1971, pp. 303, 311

6.3 Charles Kingsley on 1848

I have promised to say little about the Tenth of April, for indeed I have no heart to do so . . . We had arrayed against us, by our own dread folly, the very physical force to which we had appealed. The dread of general plunder and outrage by the savages of London, the national hatred of that French and Irish interference of which we had boasted, armed against us thousands of special constables, who had in the abstract little or no objection to our political opinions . . . Above all, the people would not rise . . . they did not care to show themselves. And the futility after futility exposed itself. The meeting which was to have been counted by hundreds of thousands, numbered hardly in tens of thousands . . . O'Connor's courage failed him, after all.

Source: Charles Kingsley, *Alton Locke*, London, 1850, reprinted London, 1970, p. 309

6.4 R. C. Gammage – a contemporary historian – on 1848

It is evident that the spirit of unity was lacking in the Chartist body. O'Connor's policy, on the 10th of April 1848, had been the main cause of the disunion . . . O'Connor was wrong, not in abandoning the procession, but in having encouraged so long the empty braggarts, and enthusiastic but mistaken men of the Convention, and in inducing them, almost to the last moment, to believe that he would head the procession to the House of Commons. The boasting which took place on this subject, and the miserable result, inflicted a wound on Chartism from which it has never recovered. After the 10th of April, and the exposure of the National Petition, the Assembly should never have met. It was powerless for good, and made itself simply ridiculous by wasting most of its time in mere talk.

Source: R. C. Gammage, *The history of the Chartist movement, from its commencement down to present times,* Newcastle, 1894, pp. 331–32

6.5 G. D. H. Cole: a Fabian critique of 1848

The semblance of regained unity in the early months of 1848 concealed real differences as unbridgeable as ever. On the one hand, there was a revival of 'physical force' resolutions and underground projects of insurrection – in which, as usual, spies and *agents provocateurs* played a leading part. On the other, there were Chartists such as O'Brien, who had once been 'physical force' men, but were now not prepared to countenance any threat of revolutionary activity . . . The great day, April 10, which had been supposed to mean revolution, passed off without anything at all happening; and many people in all classes were prompt in drawing the moral that, as an aggressive force in politics, Chartism was dead . . . The events of 1848 also ended the period of O'Connor's ascendancy in the Chartist movement.

Source: G. D. H. Cole, *Chartist portraits*, London, 1941, pp. 332–33, 334

6.6 John Belchem: a revisionist perspective on 1848

By the end of 1848 O'Connor looked upon himself as the leader of a labour movement at its highest stage, directing the public mind towards a programme combining the traditional radical political catechism, with a practical scheme for social regeneration. Rash political behaviour, visionary social theories, spurious middle-class schemes were all proscribed. Throughout the year he had been striving to lead Chartism in this direction, although in the early months he had willingly adopted the requisite bellicose posture for the policy of forcible intimidation. His abjuration of the National Assembly, coming so unexpectedly and devastatingly after his militant stance in the Convention and his fortitude on 10 April, certainly impaired the Chartist leadership. O'Connor, however, can hardly be held responsible for the decisive defeat of the mass platform in 1848. Nor should he be excluded from studies of the Chartist epilogue, that protean period of radical reappraisal necessitated by the total failure of 1848. An incomparable leader of mainstream popular radicalism, O'Connor became acutely aware of the inadequacy of the mass platform. The experience of 1848, of course, convinced everyone of the inefficacy of traditional tactics. This did not necessarily occasion shamefaced retreat, although a good number could no longer resist the middle-class embrace. The renunciation of the mass platform was both the proximate cause of the 'Charter and Something More' and a necessary precondition of mid-Victorian 'consensus and cohesion' . . . in the late Chartist period, O'Connor played what can best be described as a central role, leading the way in calling for a redirection of radical endeavour and in denouncing the great capitalists and their aristocracy of labour, yet refusing to sanction socialism and always keeping the option open for an alliance with the 'veritable middle classes'.

Source: John Belchem, '1848: Feargus O'Connor and the collapse of the mass platform', in James Epstein and Dorothy Thompson (eds.), *The Chartist experience: studies in working class radicalism and culture, 1830–1860*, London, 1982, pp. 302–3

Document case-study questions

1 6.1 and 6.2 provide a negative image of O'Connor's role in 1848. In what ways?

2 In what respects does 6.3 support the conclusions drawn by Lovett (6.1) and Cooper (6.2)?

3 6.3 comes from a novel. How far does this reduce its value for historians?

4 Gammage, in 6.4, provides important reasons why O'Connor's actions were wrong in 1848. How far are his conclusions supported by 6.1, 6.2 and 6.3?

5 Cole (6.5) concluded that after 10 April 'Chartism was dead'. In what respects was this a premature diagnosis?

6 Belchem's view of O'Connor (6.6) is far less negative than those expressed in the other sources. How convincing do you find his conclusions?

7 How far were O'Connor's calls for 'social regeneration' in 1848 motivated by the needs of the Land Plan?

8 Was O'Connor the villain or the hero of 1848? Justify your conclusions.

Notes and references

1 Dorothy Thompson, *The Chartists: popular politics in the Industrial Revolution*, Aldershot, 1984, p. 295.

2 J. T. Ward, *Chartism*, London, 1973, allocates a mere 25 pages to the period from 1842 to 1847, while Thompson, *The Chartists*, has less than 10; both include discussions of the Land Plan. The study by Preston Slosson, *The decline of the Chartist movement*, New York, 1916, though dated, is still essential.

3 Ward, *Chartism*, p. 169.

4 Ward, *Chartism*, p. 167.

5 In his *The lion of freedom: Feargus O'Connor and the Chartist movement, 1832–1842*, London, 1982, James Epstein relegates O'Connor's role after 1842 to a short, three-page postscript.

6 *The trial of Feargus O'Connor and 58 others at Lancaster*, Manchester, 1843, is the most accessible – if partisan – contemporary account, while F. C. Mather, *Public order in the age of the Chartists*, Manchester, 1959, provides a broader context.

7 John Belchem, *Popular radicalism in nineteenth-century Britain*, London, 1996, p. 87.

8 On the radical critique of machinery, see Maxine Berg, *The machinery question and the making of political economy, 1815–1848*, Cambridge, 1980, pp. 269–90, especially pp. 287–89.

9 A. R. Schoyen, *The Chartist challenge: a portrait of George Julian Harney*, London, 1958, is an outstanding biography of this seminal leader.

10 The problem of an alliance between radical organisations and trade unions is best approached in John Belchem, 'Chartism and the trades, 1848–1850', *English Historical Review*, vol. 98 (1983). This examines the development of the National Association of Organised Trades for the Industrial, Social and Political Emancipation of Labour (NAOT), an organisation of depressed trades encouraged by the Charter-socialists, and its rejection of the craft exclusiveness of the National Association of United Trades.

11 On these processes, see Eric Hopkins, *Working-class self-help in nineteenth-century England*, London, 1995, especially pp. 27–52, 95–118 and 203–22.

12 Lucy Brown, 'The Chartists and the Anti-Corn Law League', in Asa Briggs (ed.), *Chartist studies*, London, 1959, remains the major study of this issue.

13 R. C. Gammage, *The history of the Chartist movement, from its commencement down to the present times*, 1st edn, London, 1855, 2nd edn, Newcastle, 1894, pp. 270–72.

14 While Gammage's view of O'Connor's pragmatism may be valid, his analysis of the reasons for the success of the League is not. Peel's decision to repeal the Corn Laws was motivated less by pressure from the League than by the need to find a solution to the problems of the famine in Ireland. In his resignation speech he went out of his way to acknowledge his debt to Cobden. This has tended to muddy the historical waters.

15 Richard Brown, *Church and state in modern Britain, 1700–1850*, London, 1991, pp. 530–43 deals with the 'mid-century crisis'.

16 Joy MacAskill, 'The Chartist Land Plan', in Briggs (ed.), *Chartist studies*, and A. M. Hadfield, *The Chartist Land Company*, Newton Abbot, 1970, remain the only extended discussions. Malcolm Chase, '"We wish only to work for ourselves": the Chartist Land Plan', in Malcolm Chase and Ian Dyck, *Living and learning: essays in honour of J. F. C. Harrison*, Aldershot, 1996, is invaluable in bringing them up to date.

17 Gammage, *History of the Chartist movement*, pp. 249, 268, 276–78, 375.

18 Mark Hovell, in *The Chartist movement*, Manchester, 1918, thought it was 'not a real Chartist scheme', while A. L. Morton, in *A people's history of England*, London, 1938, thought it 'took up energy that might have been better spent'.

19 R. K. Webb, *Modern England*, London, 1980, p. 262.

20 Malcolm I. Thomis, *The town labourer and the Industrial Revolution*, London, 1974, pp. 99–100.

21 Chase, '"We wish only to work for ourselves"', p. 135.

22 Malcolm Chase, 'The people's farm': English radical agrarianism, 1775–1840, Oxford, 1988, is the best general survey of this issue. More specific consideration of the issue can be found in Ian Dyck, William Cobbett and rural popular culture, Cambridge, 1992, especially pp. 107–52, and P. M. Ashraf, The life and times of Thomas Spence, Gateshead, 1983, pp. 120–45.

23 Epstein, The lion of freedom, pp. 256–57.

24 See the discussion in Chapter 2, pp. 31–32.

25 Alan Little, 'Liverpool Chartists: subscribers to the National Land Company, 1847–48', in John Belchem (ed.), Popular politics, riot and labour: essays in Liverpool history, 1790–1940, Liverpool, 1992, pp. 247–51.

26 E. Yeo, 'Some problems and practices of Chartist democracy', in James Epstein and Dorothy Thompson, The Chartist experience: studies in working class radicalism and culture, 1830–1860, London, 1982, provides an invaluable examination of the legal obstacles to the registration of the National Co-operative Land Company.

27 On Jones, see John Saville, Ernest Jones, Chartist, London, 1952.

28 Epstein, The lion of freedom, pp. 270–71.

29 Roger Swift, The Irish in Britain, 1815–1914: perspectives and sources, London, 1990, is a brief general survey which is invaluable for setting the issue in context. D. Thompson, 'Ireland and the Irish in English radicalism before 1850', in Epstein and Thompson (eds.), The Chartist experience, J. H. Treble, 'O'Connor, O'Connell and the attitudes of Irish immigrants towards Chartism in the north of England, 1838–48', in J. Butt and I. F. Clarke (eds.), The Victorians and social protest, Newton Abbot, 1973, R. O'Higgins, 'The Irish influence in the Chartist movement', Past and Present, no. 20 (1961), and John Belchem, 'English working-class radicalism and the Irish 1815–50', in Roger Swift and Sheridan Gilley (eds.), The Irish in the Victorian city, London, 1985, are the best guides to the controversy about the extent of Irish involvement in popular radicalism in England.

30 On O'Connell's policies during the late 1830s and 1840s, see Oliver MacDonagh, The emancipist: Daniel O'Connell, 1830–1847, London, 1989. Unfortunately, this is disappointingly thin on relations between the association and the Chartists.

31 There are important parallels between Lalor's idea of 'moral insurrection' and his notion of an agrarian general strike and the ideas of the Chartists in 1842. James S. Donnelly, 'A famine in Irish politics', in W. E. Vaughan (ed.), A new history of Ireland: volume V, Ireland under the Union I, 1801–1870, Oxford, 1989, pp. 365–66 provides a convenient summary of Lalor's ideas.

32 H. Weisser, British working-class movements and Europe, 1815–48, Manchester, 1975, provides the best general view of radical attitudes. David Jones, Chartism and the Chartists, London, 1975, pp. 159–68, gives a more focused discussion, while F. C. Mather (ed.), Chartism and society, London, 1980, pp. 119–37, provides useful sources.

33 On Urquhart, see the elegant essay by A. J. P. Taylor, 'Dissenting rivals: Urquhart and Cobden', in his work The trouble makers: dissent over foreign policy, 1792–1939, London, 1957, and Richard Shannon, 'David Urquhart and the foreign affairs committees', in P. Hollis (ed.), Pressure from without in early Victorian England, London, 1974.

34 On the development of Lovett's internationalist stance, see Joel Wiener, William Lovett, Manchester, 1989, pp. 108–13.

35 On radical reaction to the 1848 revolutions, see Margot C. Finn, After Chartism: class and nation in English radical politics, 1848–1874, Cambridge, 1993.

36 John Saville, 1848: The British state and the Chartist movement, Cambridge, 1987, p. 1.

37 G. Claeys, Citizens and saints: politics and anti-politics in early British socialism, Cambridge, 1989, p. 208.

38 By the 1830s, the term 'socialist' had become synonymous with 'Owenite'. I have used both terms interchangeably in this section.

39 On Owenism, the most valuable study is still J. F. C. Harrison, *Robert Owen and the Owenites in Britain and America*, London, 1969.

40 Jones, *Chartism and the Chartists*, p. 37.

41 Claeys, *Citizens and saints*, pp. 268–69.

42 Three important books have resulted in a thorough revision of how historians have viewed that climactic year: David Goodway, *London Chartism*, Cambridge, 1982; Henry Weisser, *April 10: challenge and response in England in 1848*, New York, 1983; and Saville, *1848: the British state*.

43 John Belchem, '1848: Feargus O'Connor and the collapse of the mass platform', in Epstein and Thompson (eds.), *The Chartist experience*, is the clearest account of these developments and I have drawn heavily on his analysis.

44 *Northern Star*, 15 January 1848.

45 Belchem, '1848', p. 276.

46 Belchem, '1848', p. 279.

47 *The Times*, 10 April 1848.

48 Belchem, '1848', p. 282.

49 Belchem, '1848', p. 282.

50 *The Times*, 31 May 1848.

7 'The Charter and something more'

R. C. Gammage may have been technically a little premature when he travelled round the country during the 1850s lecturing on the movement's failure. Chartism persisted for a further decade, displaying vigour in some areas like Halifax, but it had effectively ceased to be a mass movement. Nevertheless, its journals still flourished and Ernest Jones and his 'Charter socialism' achieved some support, especially in London among craftsmen who were resentful about the growing influence of trade unionism. Chartists continued to be active in local politics, but by 1860 organised Chartism was dead. The last Chartist convention gathered in 1858 and two years later the NCA was formally wound up. This view of Chartism's decline during the 1850s is reflected in the writings of historians. For J. T. Ward, it was a 'finale',[1] for A. R. Schoyen, a 'retreat'[2] and for David Jones, the 'last days'.[3] This final chapter considers three questions.

1 In what ways was the radicalism of the 1850s a continuation of that of the 1840s?
2 What happened to Chartism during the late 1840s and 1850s?
3 Why did Chartism fail to achieve its objectives?

A bourgeois working class?

Soon after the mass meeting held at Kennington Common on 10 April 1848, Ernest Jones addressed these hopeful words to his Chartist supporters: 'Chartists, what is your duty? It is to organise. I tell you we are on the very verge of triumph. The Government are without funds – their expenditure is increasing . . . the middle class mistrust them – the working class despise them.'[4] To both government and employers, dissatisfied working people posed a problem and a threat. Repressive laws and vigorous policing could control their activities, and their political attitudes had been confronted, and defeated, in 1848. Yet their continuing presence in British society after the 1840s could not be ignored. Constraining working-class aspirations was possible, but it proved more effective to gain their consent to what was, after 1850, a remarkably conservative establishment. The result was an unquestionable change in the nature of working-class action, which was so fundamental that it gave the labour movement a reformist character of some permanence.[5] What was the character of this change and why did it occur? How did it affect Chartism?

The economic factor

The growing prosperity of the economy played a central role in this develop-ment.[6] During the early 1840s, economic depression had been exceptionally severe. It was, however, succeeded by high levels of investment, a boom in railway building and banking, and commercial reforms; these led to a vigorous upswing in the economy. Unemployment increased significantly in the last quarter of 1847 and the first half of 1848, however, as the economy was hit by a quite serious commercial crisis. Had it not been for the European revolutions of 1848, the return to upward growth would have occurred earlier. Business and commercial activity ran more smoothly during the third quarter of the century than before; employment generally improved, although full employment was only achieved in exceptional years. William Gladstone, in his 1863 budget, indicated the scale of growth: he stated that the national income had increased by 20 per cent between 1853 and 1861, and that the real wealth of the working class had grown to an extent previously unparalleled in Britain or abroad. It would be concurring with economic determinism to suggest that changes in the political attitudes of working people were brought about solely by greater regularity of work and rising living standards. While there may be something in the oft-quoted words of William Cobbett, 'I defy you to agitate a fellow with a full stomach', as John Saville says: 'These were without doubt important contribu-tory factors, but there is no simple causative analysis that can be offered for the historic fracture in working-class political consciousness which followed 1848.'[7]

Many of the features of the working-class reformism that dominated the decades after 1848 can be seen before 1850: there was, for example, already a significant growth of those working-class organisations that Saville calls 'defensive'.[8] Friendly societies and trade unions found an increasing role among skilled workers; co-operative activity developed after 1844. Owenite and more fully fledged Chartist activities did not so much relinquish their ideals during the 1850s and 1860s as find them increasingly less applicable to the personal situations of working people. Class conflict did not suddenly become a thing of the past, as the 1852 lockout in the engineering industry and the Preston textile strike in 1854 demonstrated. However, the political and social reforms of the 1830s and 1840s, such as the 1844 and 1847 Factory Acts and the reform of the Poor Law in 1847, brought the traditional ruling class and owners of capital into different degrees of accommodation with the working class. It was the continued diversity within the working population that played a dominant role in this process. During this period, Britain was still a long way from having a factory-based proletariat; the skilled artisan in his workshop remained the predominant working-class figure. This can be seen, for example, in mid-century Birmingham and Sheffield, both hives of small-scale producers. Such working conditions did not lend themselves to mass movements that were united in the cause of radical social change. More important to working-class people were issues of self-respect, individual reliance and self-help, while status within the local community was more relevant than social class. Engels was not alone in complaining that 'the British working class is becoming more and more bourgeois'.[9]

Social control

The establishment had some success in using different forms of 'social control' for maintaining its dominance over the working population. The influence of nonconformity tended to encourage quietism in the political arena, and the influence of religious and moral campaigns like temperance on many groups and occupations during the 1840s and 1850s should not be underestimated. It can be argued that the mid-Victorian working class was subjected to a ceaseless barrage of propaganda from both public and private agencies on behalf of a value system that supported capitalism and the ideals of self-help, laissez faire, sobriety, respectability and the mutual interests of labour and capital. Recreation became increasingly 'rational': direct action was taken to stamp out gambling, working-class blood sports, illicit drinking and overt prostitution. Constant surveillance on the part of the police was normally sufficient to drive socially undesirable activities off the streets and into remote rural areas, or behind closed doors. Heavy drinking was another activity which came under attack and more respectable alternatives were developed, such as social clubs. When Henry Solly, previously a Chartist leader, founded the Club and Institute Union (a working men's club) in 1862, he said in his letter of appeal for funds that 'it would be as reasonable to expect the heathen world to convert itself to Christianity as to expect the great bulk of the working men to give up the public house and establish private Clubs, without some impulse and guidance from those above them'.[10] There was considerable middle-class support for, and involvement in, Solly's movement and by 1867 he had set up some 300 clubs, all of them temperance establishments. Mechanics' Institutes, which had been established as early as 1823 to provide a broadly technical education for the working class, played an important role in providing educational and recreational activities, as well as being a useful medium for transmitting middle-class values; many of the 1,200 institutes that existed by 1860 enjoyed significant middle-class assistance. The Volunteer Force, which was founded in 1859 to protect Britain from foreign invasion, and which had a largely working-class membership of 200,000 by the 1870s, was a further form of social control. These organisations inculcated important standards of self-discipline into their members and led, many contemporaries believed, to a moderation of political extremism.

Social control was not, however, simply a matter of channelling working-class behaviour into the desired direction: it also involved a fundamental ideological dimension. The growth of the press, and of religion and education, played a central part in spreading the values of contemporary bourgeois society, attacking political agitation, immorality and industrial strikes, and describing the benefits of social co-operation. Literature for adults mirrored what was being read in schools; its content may have been less overtly religious, but its purpose and tone had changed little. The idea of 'taming the working classes with education'[11] can be traced back to the early years of the century, and the minutes of the Committee of the Council on Education in 1846 demonstrate a similar concern with social stability: 'Supervised by its trusty teacher, surrounded by its playground wall, the school was to raise a new race of working people –

respectful, cheerful, hard-working, loyal, pacific and religious.'[12] The evidence presented to the Newcastle Commission on Elementary Education in 1861 stressed the success of schools in transforming working-class children into 'model' citizens. For their part, working-class radicals like Lovett recognised the importance of educating the working class as a means of it ultimately achieving the franchise. Victorian religion provided a sober alternative to the public house as a centre of fellowship and general recreational activity. Both church and chapel continued to expound political and social values, preaching that people should accept their station in life, and that submission and obedience to authority were central Christian duties; Christian hymns certainly stressed the virtues of middle-class values.

There are, however, serious objections to the argument that social harmony after 1850s was the product simply of social control. Whatever the merits of the mechanics' institutes and the Volunteer Force, for example, their attraction was strictly limited: neither appears to have appealed directly to ordinary working men. By the early 1850s, in Lancashire and Cheshire, most members of the 32 mechanics' institutes were either professionals or from the middle classes. Although there may have been over 2 million children on school registers in 1861, schooling ended relatively young for most children and there was no compulsion to attend. The Religious Census of 1851 revealed the full extent of the churches' failure to attract the mass of the population, with less than half of the population attending church or chapel, and many working men despised such pious bodies as the Lord's Day Observance Society, the main instrument of Sabbatarianism (which advocated the strict religious observance of Sundays). Morally improving literature also appears to have had a restricted appeal, while the limits of the success of the temperance movement can be gauged by the fact that beer consumption reached an all-time peak in 1876 of 34.4 gallons a head consumed annually. There was some working-class support for the institutions of social control, but this came primarily from the skilled artisans.

The attack on the traditional habits and values of the working class is best seen not as an attempt by the middle class to impose its values on the working class, but as a conflict between two distinct value systems. Indeed, this conflict cut across class boundaries and united working- and middle-class 'respectables' against both the 'idle' rich and the 'undeserving' and 'idle' poor. This interpretation also has its problems, however. The 'respectability' of many working men, for example, was determined by a considerable amount of calculation and self-interest: Sunday-school attendance increased during the months before the annual treat; attendance at church might be motivated by the possibility of playing football for the church team. In this respect, the 'respectable' working class was not merely a neat, middle-class cipher; 'respectability' did not just have one meaning during the 1850s and 1860s.[13] To the middle class, it implied deference to one's 'betters', recognition of their superior virtues and attempts to copy them. To the artisans, however, it entailed a rejection of patronage and an assertion of independence. This was clearly evident in their support of Chartism during the 1830s and 1840s and their general dislike of the Poor Law and charity.

Furthermore, independence for working people did not mean the self-help philosophy preached by the middle class as popularised by Samuel Smiles, but the mutual assistance of the trade union and the co-operative society.

The extent to which the working class accepted the middle-class values of respectability is therefore difficult to measure with any degree of accuracy. Neither is it possible to assess the real impact of the different methods of social control or of the improvements in working and living conditions:

> The stabilisation of social relations was thus many-sided and gradual. It did not signal an end to class conflict or the emergence of untroubled middle-class rule . . . The shared economic experiences of workers across a wide range of trades, subjected to threats to their status and security, ensure the presence in the second quarter of the century of a working-class conscious-ness based on common struggles against excessive competition and the inequalities of capitalist market relations . . . The working class did not suddenly become liberalised or reformist . . .The mid-Victorian consensus represented a process of social stabilisation rather than class harmonisation.[14]

Perhaps the growing sense of co-operation and harmony during the 1850s and 1860s can best be explained by the passage of time. By the 1860s, there were fewer people who had had direct experience of the turmoil that characterised the Industrial Revolution. Urbanisation, industrialisation and technological change still had a long way to go, but they were familiar processes to working people.[15] People appear to have accepted that change was inevitable and, instead of attempting to turn back the clock, came to an uneasy accommodation with it. The strategies of Chartism thus lost their relevance to the aspirations and experience of ordinary working people.

Continuity or discontinuity?

The 1850s pose considerable difficulties for historians. The decade after 1848 saw the undermining of both the principles and practice of Chartism.[16] Radical protest was stifled by the increasing affluence of the economy and the growing importance of self-improvement among working people – especially the skilled artisans – while radical organisations were largely rendered ineffective by the growing confidence of the middle classes. The move to liberalism in this scenario, is seen, Miles Taylor argues, 'not as a political development but a retrograde step in class-consciousness'. Chartism during the 1850s was considered something of an afterthought and the historians of Gladstonian liberalism have largely ignored the radical politics of the 1850s. John Vincent, for example, focuses on an analysis of the Liberal Party between 1859 and 1874[17] and subsequent studies of Palmerston's governments during the 1850s and 1860s[18] regard his approach as being important because it anticipated Gladstone's style of leadership. Both Angus Hawkins and E. D. Steele accept that there was a significant degree of discontinuity in British politics during the 1850s; the politics of the 1860s was different from that of the 1840s. Radicalism declined and liberalism emerged, according to this view, because the Anti-Corn Law League was successful in 1846 and because Chartism failed in 1848.

Behind this widespread assumption is the Marxist tenet that the fundamental feature of change in capitalist societies is class struggle. The issue of working-class liberalism is explained away as an interlude between the early socialism of the Chartists and its revival in the late nineteenth century. There has, however, been an alternative viewpoint, which stresses the continuity of radical politics during the 1850s: Frances Gillespie's study of the influence of organised labour on the politics of parliamentary reform between 1850 and 1867 (published in 1927), for example, while Simon Maccoby recognises continuities in radicalism between the 1760s and 1914.[19] Historians have neglected the arguments of both; more recently, however, they have recognised that they have underestimated the extent of radical continuity between 1832 and 1867. This has occurred because of two major developments in the historiography of early Victorian politics:

1 the examination of the continuity of radical politics from the mid-eighteenth century to the mid-nineteenth century;
2 the work on liberalism between 1820 and 1850.

Gareth Stedman Jones argues that there were strong links between Chartism and the older radical critique of the political system that can be traced back to the mid-eighteenth century.[20] The main issue, he suggests, was not the denial of democratic rights or the exploitation associated with industrialisation, but the corruption inherent in uncontrolled executive power. According to Miles Taylor, the opponents of the 'Old Corruption' sought to prevent the executive (the prime minister and government) using its 'public position for private gain'.[21] The best way in which to do this, reformers like John Wilkes and James Mill argued, was to extend popular control over the executive; this, it was maintained, would make it accountable to the electorate. Stedman Jones goes further than this, and maintains that the success of Chartism during the 1830s lay in the ability of its leaders to extend this demand to include the abolition of the unequal tax burdens shouldered by the working population; this gave their cause considerable breadth and appeal. Peel's reform of indirect taxation in his 1842 and 1845 budgets (the reintroduction of income tax in 1842 and the progressive dismantling of tariffs), as well as major company and banking reforms, meant that this radical argument lost its attraction, and so, in Taylor's words, 'the movement fizzled out'.[22] This conclusion has two important implications for any examination of the 1850s. Firstly, it suggests that the success of Chartism and the radical movement in general did not depend on their class composition, or on their ability to express the interests of a single social group. Secondly, Stedman Jones has revived interest in a 'radical tradition' that remained largely unchanged between the mid-eighteenth century and the outbreak of war in 1914, despite changes in Britain's economic and social structure. At the heart of this tradition were popular governance and public accountability and responsibility. Stedman Jones and subsequent historians have thus restored politics to the radical agenda and have weakened some of the focus on class that was found in earlier work. This adjustment does not, however, go far enough in rethinking the chronology of mid-nineteenth-century radicalism. Stedman Jones still accepts that a major break occurred in radicalism in the 1840s after the critique of the 'Old Corruption'[23] lost its relevance, unlike such historians as E. F. Biagini, P. Joyce[24] and J. Vernon[25] who, although in different ways, recognise an unbroken continuity in popular politics across the Victorian period.

These differences of emphasis, Taylor suggests, may be resolved by looking at a second area of historiographical development: the new research on liberalism between 1820 and 1850.[26] This suggests that the modern Liberal Party did not emerge 'overnight' during the 1850s, but gradually developed during the decades after the Reform Act of 1832. The amalgamation of the Foxite Whig tradition with Peelite or liberal Toryism incorporated two important strands into liberalism: the Whigs brought a belief in popular government, while liberal Toryism provided a concern for 'efficient, cheap government and moral reform'.[27] The Reform Act may not have greatly increased the electorate, but it certainly strengthened the power of the House of Commons over the executive. The increase in the number of elections – especially during the 1830s – the growing number of contested constituencies, the expansion of parliamentary petitioning, and the emergence of pressure groups like Chartism and the Anti-Corn Law League, raised people's expectations of the reformed parliament. This interpretation creates a broader context within which to place radicalism between 1830 and the 1860s. The driving force behind radical politics derived not just from the radical critique of the state, as Stedman Jones suggests, but from the growing popularity of parliament and the people's desire to control the executive through the House of Commons.

These two revisionist approaches – Stedman Jones's work on the language of Chartism and new analyses of early Victorian liberalism – provide a different framework within which to consider the Chartist movement between the 1830s and the 1850s. It is clear that there were continuities in radical ideology. There was also continuity in terms of the radical personnel: the political activists who dominated the Chartist leadership in 1848 were in their early thirties or forties; many carried their radical politics into the 1850s and 1860s. Pressure-group politics also showed considerable continuity: during the 1850s, pressure groups built on the tactics of organisations like the Anti-Slavery Society, while the early experience of many mid-century activists lay in campaigns of the 1830s, like those for colonial reform and the repeal of the stamp duty. One area in which there was no apparent continuity was in political strategy: the mass platform disintegrated in 1848. But this was merely one type of political strategy; alternatives were available, and perhaps historians need to address the issue of the continuities in political strategy between the 1830s and 1850s. The focus on the mass platform and its vigorous defence by O'Connor – however justifiable – may, in some respects, make the break within radical politics in 1848 appear far greater than in fact it was.

'The Charter and something more'

It is possible to consider the development of Chartism after 1848 in several ways. Some historians, notably Dorothy Thompson and John Saville, argue that the defeat of Chartism left popular politics polarised between middle-class radicals and an increasingly apolitical working class. Others, for example Margot Finn and Gregory Claeys, suggest that the later Chartist leadership became increasingly influenced by republican and socialist ideas that were hostile to mainstream radicalism. A third approach, argued by Miles Taylor, maintains that the Chartist leadership responded to the defeat of the movement and the loss of its mass support by becoming reconciled to mainstream radical and liberal politics.

Historians face major problems in assessing the geographical influence and significance of Chartism after 1848. There are few studies of later Chartism at the local level, for example, and many contemporary writers ended their detailed accounts of the movement in 1848, while newspapers often ignored radical activities during the later period. David Jones,[28] however, cites research on Wales and the Black Country that suggests that the resilience of Chartism has been underestimated. Furthermore, in north Wales and in parts of the West Country, the movement may have entered a new phase. Chartists like A. W. Blacker of Torquay, Thomas Clewes of Stockport, Joseph Alderson of Bradford and Walter Pringle in Edinburgh continued to campaign with traditional vigour. Halifax was a particularly vibrant centre of later Chartism. On the other hand, the NCA, which had been revived in 1849, never had more than between 4,000 and 5,000 members during the following decade (and perhaps many fewer). The Chartist executive and district councils lacked financial resources. The movement disintegrated further.

In April 1848, Lovett, supported by Miall, Vincent and Robert Lowery, formed the People's League. Two days later, Cooper, Hetherington and Holyoake founded a rival People's Charter Union. Both were moderate organisations, reflecting the great pains which some Chartists took after 1848 to cast reforming politics in a favourable light. The League planned to align Chartism with an overhaul of the tax system, but soon foundered; the union became involved in reviving the agitation against the remaining stamp duty, especially after March 1849 when the Newspaper Stamp Abolition Committee (NSAC) was formed. The NSAC gained support from several prominent radicals, including Place and Holyoake, and in February 1851 became the Association for the Repeal of the Taxes on Knowledge, essentially a middle-class pressure group. The original union had already disappeared (in 1849) as a result of the failure of Cooper's plan to organise individual petitions.

The continuing newspaper taxes were of particular interest to Chartists after 1848, largely because of the large number of Chartist and radical journals which attracted duty. Despite this, Chartist literacy flourished and Gammage drew attention to the variety of publications (many often short-lived).[29] O'Brien ran the *Power of the Pence* from 1848 to 1849, and then the *Reformer* in 1850, in which he put forward his individualistic socialist views. Others produced ultra-radical journals which generally revealed a republican slant: Harney produced the *Red Republican* in 1850, for example, the *Democratic Review* between 1849 and 1851, the *Friend of the People* from 1850 to 1851 and again in 1852, and the *English Republic* between 1851 and 1855, while Jones edited *Notes to the People* between 1851 and 1852 and the *People's Paper* for six years after 1852. Passmore Edwards' *Public Good* (1850) had a pacifist flavour. Local journals also flourished, like the *Voice in the East* in Wisbech and the *Progressionist* in Buckingham, which was edited by Gammage himself. These publications reflect the intellectual maelstrom that Chartism had become, with an ever-increasing diversity of views emerging from the declining Chartist ranks.

The divisions deepen

This diversity continued to weaken the NCA, and O'Connor found his supremacy within the movement under considerable pressure. He became increasingly inconsistent and this was reflected in his frequent changes of mind;[30] he continued to be vindictive towards real and imagined enemies; he also vacillated over the question of forming middle-class alliances. In May 1849, Joseph Hume revived the call for household suffrage, or the 'Little Charter', and was roundly condemned by O'Connor; yet the following month he unsuccessfully asked Hume to adopt the People's Charter. Neither Hume's proposal in June nor O'Connor's own motion for the Charter met with widespread support in the House of Commons. O'Connor then proceeded to collaborate with the middle-class Household Suffrage Association. Such links disgusted some Chartist loyalists and further exacerbated divisions in the movement. In December 1849, a metropolitan conference consisting of 28 delegates met; it elected a provisional executive and then proceeded to argue about O'Connor's middle-class links. Harney joined O'Connor's opponents and was dismissed from the *Northern Star*; the following month he formed his own organisation, the National Reform League for the Peaceful Regeneration of Society (NRL). Existing divisions widened further, and O'Connor's remaining allies finally lost control of the NCA. In March 1850, the short-lived rival National Charter League (NCL), which favoured links with middle-class organisations, was established. O'Connor sought to keep a foot in both camps. When, on 11 July 1850 he again unsuccessfully raised the People's Charter in the House of Commons, his preamble contained clear socialist overtones. This was the last time that parliament debated the issue.

The Chartist Convention of 1851

The gulf between the Chartist leaders was now scarcely disguised. Attempts to weld the NCA, the NRL, the Society of Fraternal Democrats, the trade unions and the Social Reform League into the National Charter and Social Reform Union in 1850 failed. The major reason for this failure was the growing importance of socialism to many Chartists: Jones, for example, believed that a new unity could be achieved by socialist principles; he saw 'Charter socialism' as an organisation operating on strictly class lines against capitalism. Over-optimistic as usual, he opposed any deviation: co-operatives, trade unions, Christian socialists, 'Teetotal Chartists' and republicans were all viewed as 'sham radicals'. O'Connor was not yet prepared to relinquish control of the movement, however, and organised a conference in Manchester to create a 'perfect union'. This move provoked further division: Jones and the executive of the NCA were opposed to it, but O'Connor pressed ahead, gaining the support of a Manchester rally on 17 November 1850. The Chartist division was now clear: O'Connor and his allies stood for 'the Charter pure and simple', while Jones and his supporters argued for 'the Charter and something more'.

The Manchester conference met on 26 January 1851 and consisted of only eight delegates. It achieved nothing, although both O'Connor and Jones attended it in order to make their case. The intellectual debate had, however, left its mark and at another Chartist convention, held in the spring of 1851, the 'Charter socialists' scored a substantial victory. The convention began to assemble on 31 March in London. Many districts could not afford to send delegates, and the NCA was weakened by a number of secessions. Only 30 of the intended 49 delegates turned up and many of these lacked political experience. They rejected the 'nothing but the Charter' approach, opposed any middle-class collaboration, planned a new petition, agreed that Chartist candidates would contest the next elections (scheduled for 1853) and that the organisation would be extended to trade unions, various working groups and the Irish. These proposals were nothing new. However, the convention went on to adopt a new social programme: this sought to combine campaigning for the Charter with Poor Law reform, calls for state education, price controls, currency and taxation reform and the nationalisation of land and the mines. The convention dissolved itself on 10 April 1851, leaving the executive to restate its policies. But, as Ward comments, 'The brave new world was not to be.'[31] The NCA only had around 4,000 members and they were divided: it was not in a position to revive the moribund movement.

The role of Ernest Jones, and the demise of Chartism

Ernest Jones was the dominant Chartist figure of the 1850s. However, he never achieved the same supremacy over the movement that O'Connor had attained during the 1840s. Many found it difficult to accept Jones' innate optimism; this was already evident at the National Assembly of 1848 and became more obvious over the following years. Jones inherited a movement that was already fatally flawed: death and emigration had decimated the local Chartist leadership; some members dropped out of formal Chartism completely and turned to other movements. In the north and Midlands, for example, there were rival attractions, like the revival of the agitation for factory reform, that seemed to offer more tangible improvements for working people. Some Chartists believed that local politics provided a worthwhile substitute for success on the national stage and much Chartist method and energy was injected into the council chamber and parliamentary elections. In his fight to retain a separate Chartist identity, Jones faced considerable opposition, both from those who were prepared to 'go for less', but also from those who were opposed either to his personal vision or to Chartist politics.

The end of the movement was protracted, lasting the whole decade. Jones headed the poll in the winter elections to the NCA executive in 1851. His increasingly dictatorial manner alienated his former supporters, like Harney; even the 'left' within Chartism was divided. Jones now fought to dominate the movement. He backed a call for a convention to reorganise the movement, which met in Manchester from 17 to 21 May 1852. This proved short-lived and the movement limped into 1853. Jones urged working-class unity in support of the Preston cotton strikers in the winter of 1853 and called for a 'labour parliament' to lead an allegedly reviving Chartism. The parliament, which had some 40 members, met in Manchester between 6 and 18 March 1854. A 'mass movement' was planned but, by August, it was pointed out that as far as the mass of the population was concerned, this had been another failure, for it had failed to revive the mass platform or to gain any significant support among the working population. The elections to the executive that year appear to have been fixed; several districts refused to recognise it as a result, and what remained of Chartism was further divided. Chartist audiences declined. Jones' approach became increasingly dictatorial, explicitly so in early 1856. A final convention was held in 1858, which had 41 delegates. Jones renewed his demands for the 'six points', but both circumstances and his supporters eventually induced him to take his stand on manhood suffrage alone. The convention saw the birth of the short-lived Political Reform League (led by Joseph Sturge, which called for universal suffrage, the ballot, and adjusted constituency boundaries), and the practical end of the Chartist movement. The NCA staggered on for two more years; by 1860 Chartism was, finally, dead.[32]

Why did Chartism fail?

Repeated failure sapped the momentum of Chartism. In order to sustain the mass platform, the movement needed to maintain a widespread belief that success was possible. The events of 1839 seriously damaged its capacity to do this; the defeat of the general strike in 1842 and the crushing failure of 1848 completed the process. The widespread imprisonment and transportation of both leaders and rank and file, and the successful confrontation of mass demonstrations by central and local authorities, that characterise the three main phases of the Chartist agitation contributed significantly to the disintegration of the movement and reflected the growing confidence and enhanced efficiency of the coercive powers of the British state.[33] By 1848 the authorities had inflicted the most damaging series of psychological defeats of the century on the popular reform movement, thus bankrupting the long tradition of the mass platform. Without the physical assault made by the government on the militant sections of the Chartist leadership and also on many of the secondary leaders, the aftermath of the 1850s might have been different.

In part, this was a consequence of the fundamental organisational weakness of the movement. Lack of administrative experience and imagination was clearly exposed by the ways in which the conventions were organised and financed. The rejection of the three petitions of 1839, 1842 and 1848 showed how little parliamentary support the Chartists enjoyed. The reforming movement of 1830 to 1832 and the activities of the Anti-Corn Law League, both of which used similar tactics to Chartism to whip up outside pressure, were more successful because they could also rely on parliamentary allies; the Chartists could not. With little parliamentary backing or solid middle-class support, the movement found itself either having to give up, or to opt for less peaceful methods. This divided both the leadership and rank and file, creating dissension and a lack of tactical direction. Chartists could agree on the Charter, but their other aims were less precise: to Lancashire cotton-workers, for example, Chartism held out the prospect of economic improvement and factory reform; to the London artisans, it pointed the way to political equality. The Chartist leaders also had different objectives: for Lovett, the franchise was just part of a proposed general programme of social improvement; for Ernest Jones, Chartism was equated with socialism; O'Brien saw it in relation to currency reform and land nationalisation; and, for O'Connor, the franchise was the political counterpart of his schemes regarding land reform. The loss of momentum within the movement caused these differences to emerge as the various interest groups sought alternative ways of realising their ends. Chartism could not maintain a unity of purpose.

Economic conditions also played an important role in the Chartists' failure to maintain a unity of purpose. Although there has been a recent reaction against the simple economic arguments of earlier historians, the fundamental importance of the trade cycle should not be neglected: the difficulty of maintaining the momentum of Chartism, except in periods of greater hardship than usual, was universally recognised by contemporaries. The vibrant Chartism of 1838–40, 1842 and 1848 corresponded to downturns in the economy. Whether, as some historians have argued, this represented the 'politics of distress' is perhaps oversimplistic. However, once the economy revived, support for the movement ebbed away and Chartist unity was seriously compromised. Working-class radicals, albeit under the umbrella of Chartism, sought different solutions to their problems. In the early 1840s it was the 'New Move'; in the middle of the decade O'Connor's Land Plan. The effect of this was, however, not altogether negative. The changes that occurred in the policies and attitudes of government, in part the result of Chartism, can be seen as evidence of the movement's partial success. Chartism focused attention on social problems and on the need to tackle them; such efforts often occurred at local level and were prompted by a desire to reduce discontent and divisions within society, as well as by genuine Christian compassion. There was some liberalisation of domestic state policies during the 1840s, and this weakened the Chartist case that only a reformed parliament would improve the conditions of the working population.

A final explanation for the demise of Chartism lies in the consolidation of industrial capitalism that had occurred by 1850. During the previous half century, industrial change had aroused militant opposition among the working population, which believed that political reform alone could arrest or reverse this process. By 1850, this battle had more or less been lost, and increasingly the working population came to an uneasy accommodation with the capitalist economy. Chartism remained relevant only in places like Halifax and Bradford, where the woollen and worsted trades were still fighting a rearguard action against mechanisation. Militancy, in this scenario, was more associated with the traumas of the early stages of industrialisation than with the more mature and settled stages of industrial capitalism, when workers looked to trade unions and established political parties to advance the specific interests of the working population, activities which did not rely on massive confrontation but rather on 'respectable' persuasion. This does not alter the significance of Chartism in the shift from older forms of popular protest associated with the mass platform to the development of new ones – like collective bargaining and strikes and the use of pressure through mass organisations – that were more relevant to an industrial urban society. This was a gradual process. The urban male working class gained the vote in 1867 and many rural workers in 1884. Universal manhood suffrage, however, had to wait until 1918.

In terms of its geographical and occupational breadth and the unprecedented involvement of women, Chartism was the first organised mass movement of the working population in British history. However, it failed to harness trade union support in any formal way, except in the summer of 1842, and did not bridge the gulf between rural and urban workers. It did not mark a vital stage in the inevitable progress of organised labour. Chartism was motivated by 'knife-and-fork' issues, but was also concerned with the dignity of labour and the 'rights of man'. In this respect, it looked both back to the campaigns of the 1790s and forward to the emergence of socialism as a political force from the 1880s.

Notes and references

1 J. T. Ward, *Chartism*, London, 1973, pp. 220–34.

2 A. R. Schoyen, *The Chartist challenge: a portrait of George Julian Harney*, London, 1958.

3 David Jones, *Chartism and the Chartists*, London, 1975, pp. 171–80.

4 John Saville, *Ernest Jones: Chartist*, London, 1952, p. 106.

5 The literature on the changing, or more accommodating, attitude of the working class during the 1850s and 1860s is the subject of considerable debate. The following books are worth consulting. The standard text is F. E. Gillespie, *Labor and politics in England, 1850–67*, Durham, 1927. This should be complemented by Margot C. Finn, *After Chartism: class and nation in English radical politics, 1848–1874*, Cambridge, 1993; Neville Kirk, *The growth of working-class reformism in mid-Victorian England*, London, 1985, a study based on Lancashire; and Trygve Tholfsen, *Working-class radicalism in mid-Victorian England*, London, 1976. E. F. Biagini and A. J. Reid (eds.), *Currents of radicalism: popular radicalism, organised labour and party politics in Britain, 1850–1914*, Cambridge, 1991, forcibly stresses the continuity of attitudes across the 1850 divide.

6 On the economy of the 1850s and 1860s, see R. A. Church, *The great Victorian boom, 1850–1873*, London, 1975, a valuable bibliographical corrective to the view that these decades were, in some ways, exceptional.

7 John Saville, *The consolidation of the capitalist state, 1800–1850*, London, 1994, p. 80.

8 I take 'defensive' to mean that these organisations protected the interests of working people within the context of an increasingly capitalist economy.

9 Engels to Marx, 7 October 1858, quoted in K. Marx and F. Engels, *Selected correspondence*, Moscow, 1956, p. 133.

10 Quoted in J. Taylor, 'From self-help to glamour: the working man's club, 1860–1972', *History Workshop Pamphlet*, vol. 7 (1972), p. 2.

11 James Kay-Shuttleworth, secretary of the Committee for Education between 1839 and 1849, certainly saw education in the light of social control.

12 Quoted in R. Johnson, 'Educational policy and social control in the mid-nineteenth century', *Past and Present*, vol. 73 (1970), p. 119.

13 Adrian Jarvis, *Samuel Smiles and the construction of Victorian values*, Stroud, 1997, considers the issue of 'respectability' from a revisionist perspective.

14 Peter Taylor, *Popular politics in early industrial Britain. Bolton, 1825–1850*, Keele, 1995, p. 223.

15 Martin Hewitt, *The emergence of stability in the industrial city: Manchester, 1832–1867*, Aldershot, 1996, is a useful case study.

16 For what follows, I have relied heavily on M. Taylor, *The decline of British radicalism, 1847–1860*, Oxford, 1995, pp. 2–9.

17 John Vincent, *The formation of the British Liberal Party, 1857–1868*, London, 1966.

18 For example, E. D. Steele, *Palmerston and liberalism, 1855–1865*, Cambridge, 1991.

19 S. Maccoby, *English radicalism*, 6 vols., London, 1935–61 and S. Maccoby (ed.), *The radical tradition, 1763–1914*, London, 1952.

20 Gareth Stedman Jones, 'Rethinking Chartism', in his *Languages of class: studies in English working class history, 1832–1982*, Cambridge, 1983, pp. 90–178.

21 Taylor, *The decline*, p. 5.

22 Taylor, *The decline*, p. 5.

23 W. D. Rubenstein, 'The end of the "Old Corruption" in Britain, c. 1780–1860', *Past and Present*, vol. 101 (1983), is a useful survey of the break during the 1840s. It should now be supplemented by Philip Harling, *The waning of 'Old Corruption': the politics of economical reform in Britain, 1779–1846*, Oxford, 1996.

24 Patrick Joyce, *Visions of the people: industrial England and the question of class, 1840–1914*, Cambridge, 1991, and Patrick Joyce, *Democratic subjects: the self and the social in nineteenth-century England*, Cambridge, 1994.

25 James Vernon, *Politics and the people: a study in English political culture, 1815–1867*, Cambridge, 1993, and James Vernon (ed.), *Re-reading the constitution: new narratives in the political history of England's long nineteenth century*, Cambridge, 1996.

26 P. Mandler, *Aristocratic government in the age of reform: Whigs and Liberals, 1830–1852*, Oxford, 1990; J. Parry, *The rise and fall of Liberal government in Victorian Britain*, Yale, 1993; T. A. Jenkins, *The Liberal ascendancy, 1830–1886*, London, 1994; and T. A. Jenkins, *Parliament, party and politics in Victorian Britain*, Manchester, 1996, are valuable summaries of current thinking.

27 Taylor, *The decline*, p. 7.

28 Jones, *Chartism and the Chartists*, pp. 168–69.

29 R. C. Gammage, *The history of the Chartist movement, from its commencement down to the present times*, 1st edn, London, 1855, 2nd edn, Newcastle, 1894, pp. 345–46.

30 The growing inconsistency in O'Connor's actions may well have heralded psychological problems or may have been associated with the onset of syphilis. He was eventually taken into Dr Harrington Tuke's asylum at Chiswick, convinced that he was a state prisoner. He died in 1855.

31 Ward, *Chartism*, p. 228.

32 Ward, *Chartism*, pp. 235–44, provides an invaluable discussion of what happened to the leading Chartists after the demise of Chartism.

33 John Saville, *1848: the British state and the Chartist movement*, Cambridge, 1987, considers the development of the coercive powers of the state.

Select bibliography

I have confined this brief bibliography to general references. Further bibliographical references can be found at the end of each chapter.

General surveys

Several valuable general surveys of radicalism containing information on Chartism may be consulted: E. Royle and J. Walvin, *English radicals and reformers, 1760–1848*, Brighton, 1982; E. H. Hunt, *British labour history, 1815–1914*, London, 1981; and J. T. Ward (ed.), *Popular movements, 1830–1850*, London, 1970. D. G. Wright, *Popular radicalism: the working class experience, 1780–1880*, London, 1988, and his documentary, *Democracy and reform, 1815–1885*, London, 1970, contain useful material on Chartism. Richard Price, *Labour in British society*, London, 1986, is a major interpretative study and should be contrasted with J. Belchem, *Industrialisation and the working class*, London, 1990, and also Belchem's *Popular radicalism in nineteenth century Britain*, London, 1996.

Bibliographical and reference materials

Detailed bibliographies that include references to Chartism include: D. Nicholls, *Nineteenth century Britain, 1815–1914*, London, 1978; J. L. Altholz, *Victorian England, 1837–1901*, Cambridge, 1970; L. M. Brown and I. R. Christie, *Bibliography of British history, 1789–1851*, Oxford, 1977; H. J. Hanham, *Bibliography of British history, 1851–1914*, Oxford, 1976; and W. H. Chaloner and R. C. Richardson, *Bibliography of British economic and social history*, Manchester, 1984. J. F. C. Harrison and D. Thompson, *Bibliography of the Chartist movement, 1837–1976*, Brighton, 1977, and Owen Ashton, Robert Fyson and Stephen Roberts (eds.), *The Chartist movement: a new annotated bibliography*, London, 1995, are complementary bibliographical studies. These are essential for students who want detailed bibliographical references to primary and secondary sources. E. Royle, 'Reading history: Chartism', *History Today* (December 1985), is a valuable shorter listing and should be read in relation to Hugh Cunningham, 'The nature of Chartism', *Modern History Review*, vol. 1 (1990).

Source collections

G. D. H. Cole and A. W. Filson (eds.), *British working class movements, 1789–1875*, London, 1957, is the best documentary collection. See also J. T. Ward, and W. H. Fraser, *Workers and employers*, London, 1980. E. Royle, *Chartism*, 3rd edn, London, 1996, Dorothy Thompson, *The early Chartists*, London, 1971, F. C. Mather, *Chartism and society*, London, 1980, are standard documentary studies.

Chartism: general studies

F. C. Mather, *Chartism*, London, 1965, and J. R. Dinwiddy, *Chartism*, London, 1987, are brief surveys. More detailed studies include Asa Briggs (ed.), *Chartist studies*, London, 1959; James Epstein and Dorothy Thompson (eds.), *The Chartist experience: studies in working class radicalism and culture, 1830–1860*, London, 1982; D. Jones, *Chartism and the Chartists*, London, 1975; Dorothy Thompson, *The Chartists: popular politics in the Industrial Revolution*, Aldershot, 1984; and J. T. Ward, *Chartism*, London, 1973.

Chronology

1832 Reform Act passed.

1833 Factory Act passed.

1834 *March:* Tolpuddle Martyrs sentenced.
July: Poor Law Amendment Act passed.
August: collapse of Grand National Consolidated Trades Union.

1835 Working men's associations and radical associations formed in the north and Scotland.
September: Municipal Corporations Act passed.

1836 *March:* stamp duty on newspapers reduced.
June: London Working Men's Association (LWMA) formed.

1837 *January:* formation of East London Democratic Association.
LWMA petition, containing the 'six points', drafted.
May: revival of Birmingham Political Union.
July: general election held.
November: Northern Star first published in Leeds.

1838 *April:* formation of Great Northern Union in Leeds.
May: People's Charter published in London.
National Petition unveiled in Birmingham.
August: great Birmingham rally held.
September: Kersal Moor meeting held near Manchester.

1839 *February:* Chartist Convention meets in London.
March: formation of Anti-Corn Law League.
May: Chartist convention moves to Birmingham.
July: Bull Ring Riots in Birmingham followed by arrest of Lovett and other Chartist leaders.
Chartist Convention returns to London.
National Petition rejected by House of Commons by 235 votes to 46.
August: Rural Police Act passed.
'Sacred month' demonstrations.
November: Newport Rising.

1840 *January:* failed risings in Sheffield, Dewsbury and Bradford.
February to March: Chartist trials held.
March: emergence of 'Christian Chartism' in Scotland.
July: Chartist conference held in Manchester.
Formation of the National Charter Association.
Winter: O'Connor attacks 'foreign-policy' Chartists.

1841 *Spring:* emergence of 'Teetotal Chartism'.
April: Lovett forms National Association of the United Kingdom for Promoting the Political and Social Improvement of the People.
O'Connor attacks 'Knowledge', 'Teetotal' and 'Church' Chartism.
May: Petition Convention held, followed by the defeat of the petition in parliament.
August: general election: Peel and Conservatives defeat Melbourne's Whig government.

1842 *April:* Complete Suffrage Union Conference held in Birmingham.
Chartist Convention held in London.
May: parliament rejects second National Petition by 287 votes to 46.
August to September: the 'Plug' strikes, followed by arrest of Chartist leaders.
December: unsuccessful conference of Chartist and Complete Suffrage representatives.

1843 *March:* O'Connor's trial in Lancaster.
September: Chartist Convention held in Birmingham: Land Plan accepted.
Chartist executive moves to London.

1844 *April:* Chartist Convention held in Manchester.

1845 *April:* Chartist Convention held in London.
Chartist Land Society formed.
September: Society of Fraternal Democrats formed.
December: Manchester conference held on the Land Plan.

1846 *June:* repeal of the Corn Laws.
December: Birmingham conference held on the Land Plan.

1847 *May:* O'Connorville opened.
July: general election won by Lord John Russell and the Whigs.
O'Connor elected MP for Nottingham.
August: Lowbands conference held on the Land Plan.
Factory Act passed.

1848 *February:* outbreak of revolution in France.
April: Chartist Convention held in London.
10 April: Kennington Common demonstration held.
May: National Assembly meets.
Summer: widespread Chartist disturbances and arrests.
July: Irish rising aborted by the arrest of leaders.

1849 *February:* National Charter Association revived.

1850 *January:* Harney establishes National Reform League.
Chartist executive captured by Harney and the London Democrats.
March: National Charter League established in Manchester.

1851 *January:* Chartist Convention held in Manchester.
February: bill proposed to dissolve National Co-operative Land Company.
March: Chartist Convention held in London.

1852 *May:* Chartist Convention held in Manchester.

1853 Revival of Chartist movement in spring and summer.

1854 *March:* 'labour parliament' meets in Manchester.

1858 *February:* last national Chartist Convention held.

1860 National Charter Association wound up.

Index

Adams, W. E., 48, 104
Anti-Corn Law League, 19, 33, 81, 83, 84, 91, 112, 121, 123, 128; attitude of Chartism to, 96, 97
Attwood, Thomas, 19, 41, 52, 84

Barnby, John Goodwyn, 103
Belchem, John, 9, 22, 95, 101, 106–7, 109, 112–13, 114, 115, 116
Benbow, William, 41, 56
Birmingham, 13, 56, 62, 73, 79, 80, 83, 118; and Church Chartism, 74, 75; Complete Suffrage Union and, 46, 84, 85; and first Chartist convention, 58, 59
Birmingham Political Union (BPU), 19, 52, 53, 54, 55, 57
Bradford, 24, 63, 100, 109
Brewer, Patrick, 73
Briggs, Asa, 5, 29, 32
Browning, Archibald, 73
Bull Ring riots (1839), 59

Carlile, Richard, 12
Carlyle, Thomas, 2, 20, 38–39
Catholic Church, 24, 33, 100; anti-Catholicism, 33; in Ireland, 24, 33, 100
Charter, the People's, vi, 10, 15, 23, 29, 46, 47, 51, 53, 71, 72, 83, 84, 93, 103, 105, 109, 124; creation of, 10, 53; nature of, 10, 51, 105; support for, 24, 27, 55, 103
Chartism: attitude to violence, 69; Charter socialism, 117, 125; Chartism of 'hunger', 4, 19, 24, 85; Church Chartism, 71–5, 91, 95, 103; continuity or discontinuity in 1850s, 117, 121–3, 129; culture of, 8, 82; divisions in, 54, 55, 56, 70–9, 82, 93, 128; emergence of, 10–22; and European revolutionaries, 44, 99, 101–3; failure of, 4, 6, 7, 33, 127–9; foreign-policy Chartism, 101–2; and general strikes, 25, 28, 30, 58–9, 93; geography of, 6, 23–4; government responses to, 58, 59, 62, 63, 69, 76, 93, 99, 107; 'knowledge Chartism', 43, 44, 69–71, 82; leadership of, 27, 28, 29, 38–50, 69, 93, 94, 128; mass meetings, 28, 29, 31, 52, 54, 58, 63, 105, 106, 128; membership 4, 23–37, 54, 80, 81; metropolitan Chartism, 29–31, 34–5, 104, 105, 106; moral-force Chartism, 4, 42, 43,
44, 55, 56, 70, 71, 82; municipal Chartism, 77–9, 81; 'new movers', 43, 70; petitions, 1, 24, 26, 32, 53, 54, 55, 57, 63, 85, 104, 106, 109, 128; physical-force Chartism, 4, 42, 55, 56, 57, 60, 71, 82; and religion, 24, 33, 71, 82; revolutionary threat of, 58, 59, 61, 63, 82, 102–4, 109, 110, 111; 'Teetotal Chartism', 69, 75–7, 82, 126; and 'ulterior sanctions', 44, 57, 58, 59
Chase, Malcolm, 97, 98
Church of England, 72, 95; rates, 33; tithes, 33
Claeys, Gregory, 103, 104, 124
class, 1, 118, 119, 120; agricultural workers, 24, 27, 28, 29, 32, 94; artisans or skilled workers, 3, 27, 28, 29, 30, 51, 53, 77, 96, 118; builders, 28; debate on, 1, 2, 6–7; factory workers, 24, 28, 31, 118; handloom weavers, 24, 25, 32; middle classes, 13, 28, 33, 56, 57, 69, 74, 76, 83–5; miners, 25, 32, 85, 96; nature of, 6, 29; outworkers, 24, 25, 45; sweated trades, 25, 28, 30, 51; women, 25–6, 28, 44
Cleave, John, 14, 56, 76
Cobbett, William, 1, 12, 13, 81, 118
Cobden, Richard, 34, 83, 97
Cole, G. D. H., 5, 42, 45, 48, 65, 112
Collins, John, 43, 60, 70, 73, 83
Complete Suffrage Union, 46, 74, 76, 83, 84–6, 91
Conventions, Chartist: 1839 London and Birmingham, 15, 19, 24, 29, 35, 42, 56–9; 1840 Manchester, 62; 1842 London, 30, 45, 85, 94; 1843 Birmingham, 95; 1844 Manchester, 96; 1845 London, 96; 1846 Birmingham on Land Plan, 46; 1848 London, 30, 46, 105, 107; 1851 Manchester and London, 99, 125; 1854 Labour Parliament in Manchester, 99, 127; 1858 last national Convention, 117, 127
Cooper, Thomas, 40, 45–6, 50, 87, 96, 111, 124
co-operation, 33, 82, 96, 118, 121
Cornwall, 24, 72, 75
Cuffay, William, 41, 107

Democratic Friends of all Nations, 44, 102
Dickens, Charles, 2
Disraeli, Benjamin, 1, 8